Nassau J. Senior

The Trades' Unions of England

Nassau J. Senior

The Trades' Unions of England

ISBN/EAN: 9783744726023

Printed in Europe, USA, Canada, Australia, Japan

Cover: Foto ©ninafisch / pixelio.de

More available books at **www.hansebooks.com**

THE TRADES' UNIONS OF ENGLAND.

BY

M. LE COMTE DE PARIS.

TRANSLATED UNDER THE AUTHOR'S DIRECTION BY

NASSAU J. SENIOR, M.A.

EDITED BY

THOMAS HUGHES, M.P.

LONDON
SMITH, ELDER AND CO., 15, WATERLOO PLACE.
1869.

AUTHOR'S PREFACE.

We owe a word of explanation to the reader who takes the trouble of perusing these pages. They may appear full of special details; the subject itself will doubtless seem altogether technical. But we hope that he, like ourselves, will see that there is a general and immediate interest in this question, which we, for our parts, have spent much time in investigating.

In speaking of the work accomplished by the masons, the iron-workers, or the tailors, and in examining scrupulously the financial organization of their Unions, we do not undertake to write either an essay on industry or a table of statistics. Our object will be to study, without prejudice, a subject which it is important to discuss from an exclusively practical view. We take great interest in following the development of Trades'

Unions, because it is necessary, on the one hand, to face without illusion the dangers which may arise from a state of things henceforth inevitable; and, on the other hand, because we are convinced that in spite of these dangers their development may be useful, not only to those who expect from it a legitimate bettering of their condition, but also to society at large. We think that this new application of the prolific principle of association will not only cause material profit and an increase of general wealth, but will also yield to society through its moral influence still more important services. It will help to remove the specious and fatal notion that the interests of capital and labour are opposed. We shall show these, the two elements of public prosperity in every country, at one time engaged in an unnatural struggle, at another time, on the contrary, regaining all their influence by a happy alliance.

The examples we shall produce will, we hope, prove how completely these elements are bound together, and then, perhaps, our labour will not have been in vain. When a ship is overtaken by fog in the midst of breakers, soundings are taken incessantly, and the smallest objects brought up by the lead from the bottom are carefully examined as a guide for the course to be taken. In the midst of the uncertainty which envelops the future of France, we cannot take too frequent soundings in the track of our neighbours, whose course is beset by the same dangers as ours. But if these inquiries are to be of any use, we must take into consideration all the details which can throw light upon this important question, which affects us as much as them.

Having, in the course of this inquiry, seen how institutions work in a free country, we have done our best to make an impartial use of the right, common to every one, of judging acts which have been the subject of public discussion between the parties interested. We hope we have succeeded in doing justice both to the powerful manufacturers, who by their intelligence contribute to the real progress of civilization, and also to the honest and laborious working-class, whose steadfast qualities are the strength and the honour of all great nations.

LOUIS PHILIPPE D'ORLEANS.

Twickenham, March 15, 1869.

EDITOR'S PREFACE.

The book, a translation of which is here given to English readers, was first published in Paris in the spring of this year. It has already passed through six editions in France, and a German translation is in the press. These facts alone would surely make it well worth the attention of those who are studying the labour question here, in the country which has furnished the subject discussed in its pages. Even if its success across the Channel is set down to the name of the author, the case is not altered. It is not every day that we find young men of the very highest rank ready to undergo the severe, and somewhat tedious, labour of endeavouring to master the greatest and most difficult problem of our time. Many of us, who have been long engaged in the same study, are well aware

—and, I hope, are always ready to acknowledge—how much they owe to members of the French emigration of 1848 and 1851 for the light which their experience has cast on many sides of the labour question in England. Hitherto, however, that light had come from political writers, or students of the professional or working-classes, such as M. Louis Blanc or M. Nadaud. It must be now admitted that the balance has been set right, and that the French royal family has earned an equal claim to our gratitude. And this on two grounds : first, because the Count of Paris's book is in itself a very valuable contribution to the English literature on this great controversy; and, secondly, because it comes at a most opportune moment, when the attention of Parliament is to be called once again, after a lapse of nearly half a century, to the state of our law respecting combinations of members of the working-class for the purpose of influencing the labour-market.

The testimony of a foreigner, if only he brings with him patience, and a clear head to the study of this question, is in some respects worth more than that of any Englishman of equal ability. At home we are all more or less biassed by our sympathies and associations; or, if not in fact so biassed, shall certainly never get the credit of strict impartiality from those who take the opposite side. If any men could claim such immunity surely Mr. Mill and Mr. Thornton might be held to deserve it: that they have not obtained it, is clear enough from the reception which has been given in many quarters to recent publications of theirs. The fairest and ablest Englishman will always be counted a partisan; foreigners who have taken a leading part in the discussion in their own country would lie under the same imputation; but in the present author we have one who brings to his work all the requisites for forming a perfectly impartial judgment. His rank places him altogether outside the controversy, while his long residence in England has made him familiar with our habits and methods of speech, and thought, and action. He is, moreover, avowedly writing for his own people, and not for us; and has no conceivable purpose to serve in England by taking one side or the other, or allowing himself any licence in deepening or shading away the colours in the picture which he has undertaken to paint of our industrial life. The question of course still remains, has he made a fair use of his peculiar position, and unrivalled opportunities? His book must answer for itself, and I at least cannot but feel that it does so, and that very emphatically, in the affirmative. In all that has been written on the subject of Trades' Unions, there is no clearer or more exhaustive summing-up in a short compass of the arguments for and against them, and of the view of the Unionists as to the objects and principles of their societies, than will be found at the end of the 4th chapter of this book. The analysis which it contains of the voluminous evidence taken by the Royal Commission on Trades' Unions is the best and most complete which has appeared, and may safely be recommended to that great majority of English readers who will never have the patience to consult the original blue-books. Here and there in his statement of the law applicable to Unions, and of the effect of some recent decisions, slight inaccuracies may be detected by those who are conversant with the subject, but such persons will be the first to admit, that on such points the gravest differences exist amongst our own most able lawyers. We should all at once allow Sir William Erle to be, if not the highest, at any rate almost the highest, authority in the realm on such questions as how far the Common Law doctrines of "conspiracy" and "restraint of trade" are applicable to combinations of employers or workmen; but we know that his conclusions have been criticized and even denied by those who have made a special study of this branch of our law. The only wonder is that a foreigner, however able and industrious, should not have made far more serious blunders when venturing (as he could not help doing) upon such technical and difficult ground.

The most interesting and valuable part of the book, however, will be found in the concluding chapters on "The Remedy for Strikes," and "The Future of Trades' Unions." Here the author is in complete accordance with the best and ablest thinkers on social subjects, amongst ourselves. Strikes and locks-out, he likens to "the Japanese duel, in which each combatant is obliged to put himself to death with his own hand." —(p. 198.) At the same time he does not attempt to deny that, under certain circumstances, they are at present as inevitable and as justifiable as the battles between regular armies. He sees as clearly as any of us that councils of conciliation and boards of arbitration, while they will assuredly decrease the number of strikes, and establish a far better feeling than at present exists between employers and their workmen, can never solve the labour question. They imply two camps, and what is needed is one only. So long as the two camps exist no system of arbitration can work satisfactorily, if, indeed, it can work at all, without some such organization as Trades' Unions—(p. 204-5). But our author looks forward to the time as rapidly approaching when the Unions will become "a new element of productive power, and an earnest pledge of peace"—(p. 197). They will prove, he thinks, "the future centre of co-operative associations"—(p. 229), and he looks upon these associations, and industrial partnerships, such as that of Messrs. Briggs (of which an excellent sketch will be found at page 214,) as the true solution of the labour question, and the end for which all social reformers should be striving.

There will of course be much difference of opinion amongst English readers as to the conclusions at which the French Prince arrives in considering the future of Trades' Unions in this country, but assuredly there will be nothing but hearty agreement and sympathy with him when he turns to his own people, with a longing, as touching as it is manly, for the time when they too may work out the problem of the future of labour by means of public meeting, free discussion, and an unshackled press. "A light, brilliant as that of the sun, and like it, composed of innumerable different shades, is needed to arrive at a right understanding of political and social questions; such a light can proceed only from the full and free expression of public opinion in all its shapes," is the end of the whole matter, for the author of this book. That such a light is beginning once again to break through rifts in those heavy clouds, "this dangerous twilight," which have so long brooded over France, must be plain enough to all who note, however carelessly, the signs of the times. We can only watch, and hope that the light may spread over that fair land, and the clouds disperse, without the terrors of a thunderstorm—the recurrence of one of those crises, to use our author's words, "when minds are disturbed, passions inflamed, and material prosperity rudely shaken." But through whatever ordeal she may have to pass before the twilight is rolled away, we may surely be pardoned for earnestly hoping that, when that time comes, the men who have spent these long dreary years of exile so honourably amongst us, be they Republicans, Royalists, Orleanists,—princes, journalists or workmen,—may find their own place again in their own land; and while they add vigour to her political life, and strength to her counsels, may retain a kindly feeling for the temporary home in which they have been able to study to such good purpose the questions which they must help to solve for France.

T. HUGHES.

Lincoln's Inn, June 19, 1869.

CONTENTS.

CHAP.		PAGE
I.	THE SHEFFIELD OUTRAGES	1
II.	I.—THE ORIGIN OF TRADES' UNIONS	21
	II.—THE LEGAL POSITION OF TRADES' UNIONS	26
III.	THE ORGANIZATION OF TRADES' UNIONS	34
IV.	THE BUILDING TRADE	54
V.	THE IRON TRADE	81
VI.	THE COAL TRADE	113
VII.	THE IRON SHIP-BUILDING TRADE	144
VIII.	VARIOUS TRADES	167
	I. *The Tailors' Trade*	169
	II. *The Glass-makers*	174
	III. *The Printers*	178
	IV. *The Cotton-Spinners*	184
IX.	THE REMEDY FOR STRIKES	194
	I. *Arbitration*	200
	II. *Co-operation*	213
	The Colliery of Briggs and Company	214
	The Assington Agricultural Society	224
X.	POLITICAL LIBERTY AND THE FUTURE PROSPECTS OF UNIONS	228
	APPENDIX	239
	POSTSCRIPT	245

THE TRADES' UNIONS OF ENGLAND.

CHAPTER I.

THE SHEFFIELD OUTRAGES.

EVERYBODY now admits the advantages which the working-classes may derive from association, and no one disputes their right to make use of it; but experience alone can teach them how to handle an instrument, which is at the same time so powerful and so delicate. Accordingly it concerns every nation to take into consideration the attempts made by their neighbours in this direction, in order to discover what should be imitated, and what avoided.

In France the logical nature of the people has led to a preference for the form of association, which is the most perfect in itself, but, at the same time, the most difficult of application, viz. co-operative societies of production. Germany is already covered with a network of those admirable institutions, savings-banks, to which Mr. Schulze-Delitsch has given his name. Lastly, in England the co-operative societies for sale, so well described by M. Jules Simon, are growing and developing themselves. These admit customers to a share in the profits of the retail dealer, thereby making it possible for the working-man, whose whole wage was before absorbed in his daily expenses, to save money.

But it is not our object to show the advantages of these different institutions; they are already well known and appreciated. We now propose to discuss another sort of workmen's associations, very powerful in England, but which neither came out under the same happy auspices, nor have since obtained among all ranks the same sympathies as the institutions above referred to. We mean the Trades' Unions, those vast coalitions of workmen which are endowed with a complete and permanent organization, and whose influence on British industry has, in these days, become so important as to be well worth our attention.

Created in the midst of the fatal struggles called strikes, they have preserved their warlike character. Accordingly, they have been both attacked and defended with equal violence. Those who most clearly see their power are those who most fear them. Attempts have been made to hold them responsible for some isolated crimes; they have been condemned without mercy for holding some erroneous economical doctrines: in short, it has never occurred to any one whether this furious charger might not be harnessed to the plough, and thus yield valuable service to Society.

But public opinion in England never confirms hasty judgments. Before deciding it insists on having all the light that serious and exhaustive discussion can throw on a subject. Special circumstances have occurred to call forth this discussion and to attract universal attention to the subject. The fact is, that, on the one hand, the Reform, by which England has enlarged the base of her national representation, will gradually invest the working-classes with great influence, and, therefore, gives new importance to everything that concerns them. On the other hand, the Government, in obedience to the unanimous wish of the nation, has intervened by promoting an inquiry, in which both parties shall be heard, into the question of Trades' Unions. A Commission of Inquiry has been appointed, composed of men holding the most opposite opinions; the result of their labours has been published faithfully every month, and has thrown a new light upon this question; and it is to the result thus obtained that we propose to direct our attention.

The origin of this inquiry may be traced back to two circumstances, which at first sight appear rather of a private nature than of public importance, but which became, through their consequences, remarkable events.

The town of Sheffield was the scene of the first. The active and populous capital of the steel manufactory is situated in the centre of England, in the neighbourhood of several coal-pits, at the bottom of a deep valley, and in the midst of smoke. The most powerful steam-hammers in England, and the immense Bessemer converters—gigantic retorts, in which five or six tons of iron are bubbling—may be seen here. Here, too, cannons and plates for ships' armour are cast. By the side of these modern inventions, cutlery, the old trade of Sheffield, thrives. The trade, however, has lost its ancient monopoly. In some of its branches it has had to stand a ruinous competition, and among them no one has suffered more than the saw manufactory. The working cutlers, who are few in number, and both jealous and exclusive, have formed Trades' Unions in every branch of the trade, hoping thereby to obtain a rise in their moderate wages. They have not succeeded, and frequent quarrels between them and their masters is the result. A workman named Fearnhough had seceded from one of these societies, the Saw-Grinders' Union, to which he belonged. In the eyes of his fellow-workmen this was deserting in the face of the enemy. On the 8th of October, 1866, a violent explosion shook the small house he occupied with his family, causing great damage; and the inhabitants escaped only by a miracle. A box of gunpowder, placed with a lighted match in the cellar, had burst against the house. The author of the crime remained undiscovered. Public opinion was the more excited because this was not the first attempt of the sort. In the course of a few years Sheffield had been the scene of more than ten similar explosions, several cutlers had fallen victims, and in not one of these cases had justice been satisfied. In 1859 a workman named Linley was killed in the middle of a room full of people by a ball, without any report, fired doubtless from an air-gun, and no one had been able to discover the assassin. As all these attacks had been directed against persons hostile to Trades' Unions, the public naturally came to attribute them to those societies. The Unions indignantly repelled this accusation. That to which Fearnhough had belonged distinguished itself beyond all the others by the zeal it displayed in helping the authorities to discover the author of the explosion of the 8th of October. Its secretary, Broadhead, even headed a subscription for increasing the reward promised to the informer; but all was in vain: the mystery was not cleared up, distrust increased, and the agitation of the public continued.

A short time afterwards, however, quite another sort of affair came to occupy public attention.

On this occasion the Unions instead of being the

objects of more or less vague accusations found themselves in the position of plaintiffs. The treasurer of one of these societies embezzled a few pounds from the cashbox. He was arraigned before the Bench at Bradford and acquitted. The magistrates decided that inasmuch as the constitution of the Union contained rules contrary to law, they could not recognize its right to hold property. The Court of Queen's Bench, on appeal, confirmed this decision on the 16th of January, 1867. This judgment fixed the law on the subject: great, accordingly, was the alarm of the Unions, who thus learned that their funds, consisting sometimes of many thousands, were at the mercy of a dishonest treasurer. It is greatly to the credit of the humble officers of these great associations that not one of them has, since this judgment, betrayed his trust.* Still the position of the Unions was unbearable; they would have either to break up, or to get their interests recognized by the law. At this juncture they requested the Crown to appoint a commission of inquiry with a view to legislation.

No delay is allowed in a free country after public opinion has once taken up a question. Accordingly by the 12th of February the Commission was appointed, and held its first public sitting in London on the

* There have been several similar attempts since the decision of Hornby v. Close, the case referred to in the text; but, on the whole, the tribute here paid by the Author has been well deserved.—*Editor's Note.*

18th of March. In the meantime, however, people called to mind the outrages at Sheffield, others were mentioned as having been committed at Manchester under similar circumstances: and the enemies of the Unions maintained that the whole system of trade societies was responsible for these crimes. It was impossible to lie under the weight of such a charge. In order to afford the Unions the means of justifying themselves, Parliament authorised the Home Office to appoint two sub-Commissions for the purpose of investigating the origin of the outrages at Sheffield and Manchester, and to facilitate this object invested them with extraordinary powers. These different Commissions, in conducting the inquiry confided to them, heard the arguments on both sides, and by their impartiality, patience, and discernment, have been of great service to England. They have enabled the public to distinguish what was good from what was evil, and to shake off more than one prejudice; and they have given the opportunity to interests supposed to be directly antagonist, of standing face to face, of offering mutual explanations, and not seldom of making some advance towards reconciliation.

Before we study the history and the organisation of the Unions as revealed in the sittings of the Royal Commission in London, it is necessary to reduce the charges which hung over them to their just proportions, and for this purpose to begin by accompanying the sub-

Commissioners in their inquiry at Sheffield and at Manchester.

The Sheffield inquiry had a singularly difficult task: it had to discover the truth where all the researches of the police had been in vain. But it was greatly assisted by the extraordinary powers it had received, which gave it the authority of a court of justice. One of the merciful rules of criminal procedure in England is that, a witness, being on his oath to declare the truth to the court, cannot, if he accuses himself, be prosecuted for a confession thus obtained. The Commission had power to grant this immunity to the witnesses called before it; and this power became in its hands a much more potent instrument than it can ever be in those of an ordinary court; because, in the first place, there was no limit to the scope of its inquiries, and also because, having no judgment to give and no prisoner to sentence, the Commission at once summoned as witnesses all those to whom the vague suspicions of public opinion pointed. If their confession was sincere and complete, the Commissioners were to give them a certificate of indemnity, specifying the crimes or offences of which they had been found guilty. If they denounced any of their accomplices, the latter could, by taking the same course, obtain the same indemnity. But a witness who in a single instance perjured himself, or who kept back any portion of the truth, was to be exposed to the utmost rigour of the law. The Commission, which was composed of three barristers (Messrs. Overend, Barstow, and Chance), opened its sittings at Sheffield on the 3rd of June, 1867. Two other barristers also attended, one of whom represented the employers, who combined to assist in the inquiry, the other the Unions, who had asked for the creation of this tribunal.

There was great agitation in Sheffield; no one believed in any discovery. But such was the tact and discretion with which the inquiry was conducted, that at the very commencement of the proceedings a corner of the veil was raised; and the double inducement held out, viz., punishment for the obstinate, impunity for confessions, soon enabled the Commission to tear it completely aside. Then during twenty-five days the strange spectacle was presented of criminals relating their misdeeds, and taking the greatest care not to omit a single detail. In some instances, after having accused themselves, they made it at first a point of honour not to betray their accomplices; but soon finding themselves compromised by subsequent passages in their evidence, if they did not tell the whole truth, they made a clean breast of it in order to obtain the promised indemnity. The secret bond which ran through all these crimes was at last discovered, the guilty came out in their true colours, and the contriver and executors of these outrages, with their accomplices, who happily were to be found among a few only of the Unions, were all brought to light. These discoveries provoked the indignation of the public, but as the truth gradually came out the vague suspicions, which had embraced the whole system of Trades' Unions, began to disperse, and at the last sitting their representative was able to declare publicly that they gloried in having joined in the call for this inquiry. There is something very striking even in the dry report of this last sitting. The offenders or their representatives appear one after the other before the Commissioners to receive their certificate, and if any one of their crimes is not mentioned in it, they call attention to it, and urgently demand its insertion. They are free henceforth, and safe from the pursuit of human justice; but if, like Cain, they are inviolable, like him, they carry on their foreheads the mark of infamy.

Such was the winding up of this strange drama. To follow the details and to understand the motives of so many crimes which had hitherto appeared inexplicable, it is necessary to know the circumstances which gave rise to them, to take into consideration the prejudices rife among the Sheffield workmen, and the passions which, gaining the mastery over perverted natures, led them on even to murder. Most of the cutlers' Unions, imbued with the spirit of monopoly, handed down to them from the guilds of the middle ages, were not satisfied with merely supporting strikes—which was the avowed object of their existence — but claimed to exercise absolute influence over the trade, to force the masters to submit to all the wishes of the majority of their members, to bring the minority under the same subjection, and for this purpose to oblige all workmen to enter their ranks. Whoever refused was considered an enemy. The Unionists looked upon independent labour, or any resistance to their tyrannical orders, as an actual sin; and most of them sincerely believed that they were treated with great injustice because the law gave them no power to punish disobedience. To take the law into their own hands was the next step, and this was constantly done. The tools of non-Unionists were secretly stolen in order to punish or intimidate them: this is called *rattening*. The victims of these thefts knew perfectly well who the authors of them were: if they resisted, the persecutions continued; but if they submitted, the secretary of the Union immediately returned the objects stolen. An immense majority who approved of these measures would have drawn back in horror at the idea of being led on into crime; but the more violent and unscrupulous among their leaders, having once transgressed the law, had no notion of being stopped by any considerations of this sort.

One of them, Broadhead, was destined to infamous celebrity. He it was who, on the occasion of the attempted assassination of Fearnhough, had made the greatest display of sympathy with the general agitation excited. The reason why the author of that attempt remained undiscovered was that Broadhead himself was guilty of it. Broadhead pointed out the victim, and paid the assassin charged with the execution of the deed. But this crime was only the last of a frightful series of outrages deliberately ordered by him, which he unfolded before the Commission. In 1854 a workman named Parker received a gunshot wound: Broadhead paid and posted the assassin. He caused the death of Linley. His principal agent, named Crookes, had received orders to wound Linley with an air-gun by way of warning. On the occasion of the first attempt the victim was hit, but the wound was considered too slight. Crookes tried again in 1859, but this time his aim was too sure, and Linley fell mortally wounded. Broadhead, after this, adopted a new system; and the explosion at Fearnhough's house was the ninth attempt at blowing up of which he admitted he was the author. Crookes, who was almost always charged with whatever had to be done, chose his own accomplices. Broadhead paid them from 4*l.* to 20*l.* for each job, according to circumstances. The expense was always charged to the funds of the Union, of which he was treasurer, for no personal enmity seems to have inspired any of these attempts: it was supposed to be for the advantage of the Union that the members of the same trade, who resisted its orders, should be persecuted. Two hundred pounds so spent figure in the accounts; some under fictitious headings, some under none at all; and not one of the persons, whose duty it was to audit the accounts, seems to have inquired how this money was spent, an evident proof of their connivance. But this connivance, instead of being dangerous to the assassins, helped them to obtain the object they had in view. The motives of the crime were intended to be apparent under the mystery which concealed the agent. In this they succeeded perfectly. The hand of the Union was always recognized; men whispered to one another that another rebel would next day be added to the list of victims, and the Union reigned by means of the terror it inspired. It might even be compared to the famous Vehm-Gericht tribunals, which pronounced judgments, the execution of which remained always enveloped in mystery.*

* Although the revelations of the Commission have opened the eyes of all those who had indirectly and involuntarily encouraged these crimes by approving of the minor persecutions directed against non-Unionists, and although they have inspired a wholesome fear in those who might now be disposed to renew these attempts, nevertheless some of the Unions who were most compromised in these deplorable affairs have shown the spirit which animates them by openly defying public opinion and morality. The Saw-handle Makers' Union persists in retaining as Treasurer a man who confessed to having contributed £7 10s. towards payment of the would-be assassins of Fearnhough. It is therefore to be feared that this system of murders has not been entirely abandoned. But if any fresh crimes similar to those already perpetrated, and whose origin is now well known, should unhappily have to be added to the list, it will not excite public opinion to the same degree

Broadhead, however, found rivals in other Unions; two murders, and fifteen attempts at personal violence and blowing up, all instigated in the course of ten years by the officers of the different Unions, were brought under the notice of the Commission; and if it has not been proved that the Unions themselves, as a body, were privy to these outrages, it is only because for the most part they made haste to destroy their books, which, doubtless, contained compromising evidence against them.*

The Manchester Commission of Inquiry sat fifteen days, from the 4th to the 21st of September. The crimes and offences, into the origin of which it had to inquire, were almost all caused by quarrels between the working brickmakers and their employers. Attacks were directed more frequently against the property than against the persons of the masters, in order to intimidate those among them who resisted the will of the Unions. Horses had their throats cut, cows were poisoned, hay-ricks burnt, brick-kilns destroyed; and it was only in the nocturnal fights arising out of these guilty acts, that one murder and numerous acts of violence were committed. The Stockport Brickmakers'

as before; nor will those, whose innocence has been proved by the Commission, be held answerable for them.—*Author's Note.*

* All these societies except one, that of the Brickmakers, are formed out of the different branches of the cutlery trade.—*Author's Note.*

Union was the only one convicted of having openly countenanced these depredations. Some others virtually admitted their guilt by destroying the evidence which might have compromised them. One of these, for instance, refused to deliver up its books : in the end, the five chests in which the books were kept were seized, and brought in triumph before the Commission : the treasurer was allowed twenty-four hours to come and open them, and then they were broken open. The chests were empty ! Either before or after the seizure some skilful hand had withdrawn all the documents contained in them. Public opinion pointed to one Kay, as the leader in, and contractor for, these nocturnal expeditions, by which he was said to make a good living; but, as he had no wish to imitate the cynical confessions of Broadhead, he disappeared from Manchester ; and, by so doing, confirmed the revelations about to be made by his accomplices. Nevertheless, with these exceptions, the only fault to be found with the Manchester Brickmakers' and Masons' Unions, is that, by their absurd trade rules, they encouraged a feeling of hostility on the part of the workmen towards the masters, which led several members of them to commit the deeds of violence we have just mentioned.

We have dwelt thus long upon the unpleasing aspects of our subject, because we are persuaded that in approaching the examination of an institution such as that we are now studying, it is most necessary to keep the eyes open to all possible dangers that may arise from it. But we should not have undertaken this work had we not thought that it would give us an opportunity of showing how far only the evils of the system extend, and also of correcting once for all much exaggeration. In writing of Trades' Unions we shall have to mention some more isolated deeds of violence, to blame many more errors, many prejudices, much abuse of the power of combination; but we believe that men of impartial minds, and insensible to false alarms, will see in these excesses no motive for pronouncing unqualified condemnation on a vigorous institution, which is as yet only groping for and feeling its way.

No party spirit entered into the composition of the Royal Commission. It contained all the materials for a complete and exhaustive discussion; for its members, ten in number, under the presidency of Sir William Erle, one of the most honoured judges of England, held the most opposite opinions. The House of Lords was represented by Lord Lichfield, distinguished for the part he took in endeavouring to reconcile the ironmasters with their men in 1865. The House of Commons supplied four members, only one of whom, Sir Daniel Gooch, a director of the Great Western Railway, and best known for the important part he took in laying the Trans-Atlantic Cable, was a supporter of the Government; the three others were Lord Elcho, a Liberal Conservative; Mr. Roebuck, the eloquent lawyer, an Independent Radical; and Mr. Thomas Hughes, the popular writer, professing democratic opinions. To these were added Mr. Harrison, a barrister, the intimate friend of Mr. Hughes; Sir Edmund Head, ex-Governor-General of Canada; Mr. Booth, Mr. Merivale, one of the under-secretaries in the India Office, and Mr. Mathews, ironmaster, as the representative of the great trade interest. Divergencies of opinion showed themselves from the very beginning at the meetings, and even in the questions put to the witnesses summoned. As each member had the right of asking questions, the witnesses always found themselves, after their first, or examination in chief, subjected to a cross-examination put by some Commissioner anxious to criticise the value of their evidence, and to make out its weakness, where it happened to tell against his own views. Accordingly the commission, which has not yet ended its labours, will probably be eventually divided in opinion, and will not be able to agree in signing an unanimous report;* but surely this is much better than if the inquiry had been conducted in a one-sided

* This prediction was verified. Lord Lichfield and Messrs. Hughes and Harrison sent in a separate Report, and Lord Elcho and Mr. Merivale, while signing the Report of the majority, expressed their dissent from it on important points.—*Ed.*

manner, which would have destroyed all its influence. During this long procedure, which has lasted nearly two years, the Commission listened to witnesses of all classes and all professions. Masters and workmen have been called to appear before the same bar; in fact both masters and workmen anticipated their summons. The representatives of the Unions would, of course, be the first to come and set forth their position and their wishes; the masters who had suffered from strikes would not fail to appear and answer them. Both sides endeavoured to obtain auxiliaries in the opposite camp. The masters, hostile to the Unions, produced workmen who alleged that they were victims of the societies. The men, who lived on amicable terms with their employers, expected their masters to give evidence favourable to the Unions. By obliging both sides to state clearly their grievances, to set forth their objects, and to listen calmly to one another, instead of indulging in vague recriminations, the Commissioners were enabled to soothe animosities, and to accomplish a much more important and lasting work than any laws they might have been instrumental in passing. With all their zeal they could not, by means of the oral testimony submitted to them, grasp the immense field of inquiry open to them. They therefore resolved to confine themselves, first, to studying the principal types common to all Unions, and which have been universally recognized as the model on which the system should be organized; next, to examine thoroughly into the struggles which have distracted some of the most important trades in England. With these objects the Commission selected four trades: the building, the iron-working, the coal-mining, and the ship-building trades; and finished its labours by inquiries upon the subject of the solvency of Trades' Unions, the tailors, glass-blowers, and printers' strikes, and the formation of Councils of Arbitration. Lastly, besides the ten folio volumes, containing the report of forty-eight long sittings, in the shape of twenty thousand questions and as many answers, the Commissioners have published other documents: at their request the great manufacturers and the representatives of the principal Unions have filled up a form comprising the most important subjects to which their labour was directed; and Lord Stanley has collected and published a series of despatches by the representatives of England abroad, containing much valuable information on the subject of the Trades' Unions in the different countries to which they relate.

The Royal Commission, therefore, has furnished all the materials necessary for the study of Trades' Unions in England. We have only to follow it step by step guided by its impartial and patient researches. The work may at times prove somewhat hard, and we begin by craving our readers' indulgence. We shall take things in the order in which we find them arranged in the proceedings of the Commission; this will lead us to describe the working of a great number of strikes one after the other, which may, we fear, be sometimes monotonous for our reader: but it is absolutely necessary if we wish to discover the profound differences, which, under an apparent uniformity, distinguish each one of these struggles from any others of them, and to understand the various bodies of workmen who maintained the contest.

CHAPTER II.

I.—THE ORIGIN OF TRADES' UNIONS.

THE claim to regulate the rate of wages, without reference to the variations in the labour-market, which is the charge now-a-days urged against Trades' Unions, is a legacy from the legislature of the middle ages; and it was expressly in order to resist this tyranny that the first workmen's combinations were formed. Therefore, in order to trace their origin, we must for a short space go back to the period of these oppressive laws.

The terrible plague of 1348 carried off one-quarter of the population, and plunged the remainder into a state of frightful misery; but, as is generally the case in the course of human affairs, the evil brought its own remedy. The scarcity of labour soon increased its value, and would have secured to the survivors the means of retrieving their losses, had not Parliament taken the alarm and intervened. Parliament wanted to restore the same scale as had prevailed before the ravages of the disease, and thought by fixing a maximum rate of wages to escape one of the most fatal consequences of the plague. Its successors in the generations following went still further in the same path, and laws were passed more and more restrictive. In order to balance the maximum imposed on the artisans, it became necessary also to fix a maximum value on raw material and on articles of consumption, in order that the price of these might be within the means of the artisans. Next, it became necessary to protect them against competition, by putting every sort of obstacle in the way of those who wished to join their ranks: thence arose the severe rules of apprenticeship, the latest form of slavery, which modern society has found it so difficult to get rid of. But though trade in England was subjected to the fatal system of the maximum, on the other hand it escaped the absolute monopoly which the guilds exercised in France by means of the exclusive trade privileges granted to the freemen only by the wardens of companies.* In England these privileges were for the most part limited to the particular town, and once beyond the borough boundaries labour enjoyed comparative freedom. The stagnation which has fallen upon so many old English towns is no doubt owing to this difference between

---

* In the original, "monopole .... exercé .... par les maîtrises et les jurandes."—*Translator's Note.*

the two systems. Their growth was stopped, and they fell into the state of decrepitude which has given rise to the expression of "rotten boroughs;" while, in the meantime, life and activity was spreading in mere villages, which, by reason of their recent origin, were not represented in Parliament before 1832, but which are now known by the celebrated names of Birmingham, Manchester, Leeds, &c. Trade in England, though fettered, was flourishing, and became, as it grew, more and more alive to the difficulties under which it laboured. Accordingly, secret societies for removing these obstacles and raising wages soon sprung up. Severe laws were enacted against them. Under Edward VI. any man convicted for the third time of having joined them, had an ear cut off. These societies and the laws condemning them, survived after the maximum had fallen into disuse. The last restrictions imposed on the liberty of contract were not abolished till the beginning of this century, and it was not until the year 1824 that Trades' Unions ceased to be persecuted, and that the offence of combination, which was maintained as such in France till 1864, disappeared from the English code. Nevertheless, thanks to political liberty and commercial prosperity, these societies, in the years which preceded their enfranchisement, increased to such a degree, in numbers and in strength, as to exercise a serious influence upon trade. At this time most of the outrages occurred. Their members, from being obliged to act as conspirators in preparing and managing strikes, naturally became intolerant, and had no notion of resorting to any argument but force. Deprived of the exercise of their natural rights, they bound themselves to one another by cabalistic forms, by eccentric ceremonies, and by illegal oaths. Crime increased, and there was more than one obscure predecessor of Broadhead among them. The history of the Nottingham workmen, among many others, proves that the law, which allowed them to combine openly, far from irritating their hostility against the masters, has helped to bring about the happy understanding which now prevails.

In 1811 the hosiery trade of Nottingham was at a very low ebb. The workpeople were not only badly paid, but had to give an exorbitant price for the use of the looms belonging to their employers, for whom they worked at home. The introduction of machinery, which threatened to reduce their wages still lower by competing with the system of working in their own houses, brought on an explosion. The masters, as is generally the case on such occasions, were just at this time almost ruined themselves, and therefore not in a position to make any concessions to their workmen. The result was, not a strike, but an actual insurrection. The workmen met at night in secret council, declared war against the new machinery, and organized armed bands to destroy it. All the manufactories were attacked, many of them sacked or burnt; the contagion spread to the neighbouring counties, and before long the Luddites (so called from the name of one of the leaders of these gangs) committed their ravages on a grand scale. Their secret was so well kept that they escaped for some time the most active search. They appeared at intervals during six years, notwithstanding the execution of most of the leaders. Eighteen of them were hung at York in the year 1813. From that time till 1817 they were treated with the same severity, and the penalty of death was awarded to whomsoever should be convicted of breaking a loom. At last the Luddites, hemmed in on every side, sunk into common plunderers, and, finally, disappeared. But this severe suppression brought no remedy to the sufferings of the population at Nottingham, half of whom lived in 1812 upon public relief. Then it was that numerous workmen's associations were founded in the town, which developed into Trades' Unions after the combination laws were repealed. This act of justice, however, could not destroy the hostility based on the remembrance of past wrong: it continued to exist for forty years, accompanied by incessantly renewed quarrels on the wages question. However, in the course of the last three or four years, a marvellous change has come over the former home of Luddism, now a model town, in which all England may appreciate the happy effects of reconciliation by the harmony prevailing among former enemies.

We have only to add, not to multiply examples, that several of the Unions now existing, such as those of the printers in London, and of the iron-founders in Staffordshire, date from the first years of this century, some of them under the form of associations, whose objects were lawful, others as secret societies.

II.—THE LEGAL POSITION OF TRADES' UNIONS.

As we have already observed, Parliament abolished all the combination laws in 1824; but on the masters complaining that this measure enabled the workmen to break their contracts with impunity, it was modified, so as to meet this objection, by an Act passed the following year. But even after the Act of 1824, the traces of the ancient inequality, which had so long weighed heavy on the working-classes, were by no means expunged from the statute book. For instance, the "Master and Servant Act"—by which the assertion of the master was always to be held entitled to more credit than that of the servant —was abolished only last year;* and the definition of the limits within which combination must be kept in order not to incur legal penalties is still very vague. Jurisprudence

* The "Master and Servant Act" of last year abolished the inequality in the penalties for breach of contract in the case of employer and employed. Up to that time, the workman could be imprisoned, while the master could only be fined in the first instance.—*Ed.*

itself has not yet succeeded in fixing these limits. In fact, the law connects with acts evidently criminal, such as violence and threats, " all that can act in restraint of trade," and all that it calls "conspiracy." An instance can alone make the sense of this word intelligible, which does not correspond to the ordinary meaning of the term conspiracy. The simple fact of endeavouring to persuade a workman to refrain from labour is a perfectly legitimate act; but in 1867, the leaders of the tailors' strike were declared guilty of "conspiracy," for having combined to organize a system of pickets, who confined themselves to informing the workmen that such and such a shop was under strike. Again, if a master breaks his agreement with a workman, the latter can only claim damages ; whereas, *vice versâ*, the master, besides the civil action, which is always open to him, may bring a criminal indictment against the workman, and have him condemned to three months' imprisonment.* Lastly, as we have already said, the law refuses to recognize or protect any society designed to support strikes. This last provision forms one of the principal grievances; the following circumstances gave rise to it :—

Since the Act of 1824, the formation of an Union

---

* This inequality of penalty has been abolished by the "Master and Servant Act" of 1867.—*Ed.*[1]

[[1] The author is now aware that this is the case, and the slight error in the text will be corrected in a new edition about to appear almost immediately.—*Translator's Note.*]

has no longer been illegal; but, nevertheless, these societies are not regarded as corporations, nor, like jointstock companies, invested with the right of holding property. This distinction escaped the notice of their founders. They took alarm at last, some years ago, when an Act was passed granting this privilege to mutual benefit societies, provided they were registered, and had received the approval of a public officer specially appointed for the purpose. The same privileges were granted to all other societies registered in the same manner, whose objects were not illegal; but these latter had to obtain the approval of the Home Office. The English spirit of association is far too independent to submit willingly to preliminary control, however impartial may be the authority intrusted to exert it. The Trades' Union leaders were certain of obtaining ministerial sanction for all their societies in Great Britain; but a number of these associations have spread to Ireland, and the Irish Government, it was feared, might refuse to sanction them. Two members of the House of Commons, Lord Goderich (now Earl De Grey) and Mr. Sotheron Estcourt, in concert with the representatives of the principal Unions, and especially with Mr. Allan, Secretary of the Amalgamated Engineers, had a clause drawn for insertion in the Friendly Societies Consolidation Act, then before the House, which should enable Trades' Unions to be established legally, and to be registered according to the same forms as mutual benefit societies, provided always there was nothing illegal in any of their rules. This clause, which gave rise to a keen controversy at the time in the press, was passed by both Houses. Corporate privileges on certain conditions were granted to trade societies; but high legal authorities—among them Sir Alexander Cockburn (now Chief Justice) and Baron Rolfe (afterwards Lord Chancellor, by the title of Lord Cranworth) —had, the former in consultation, the latter in giving judgment, spoken out so plainly as to lead the unionists to believe that the mere act of organizing a strike would not bring them under the dissolving powers of the Act. They thought it impossible that both Houses should, with their eyes open, pass a clause which took away from them with one hand what it gave them with the other. Believing, therefore, that they were under the full protection of the law, they were greatly astonished when, in 1867, after having spent several years in this conviction, the Court of Queen's Bench came to the decision which we have mentioned above. The reasons given for this decision increased its importance. The common law of England declares every engagement "opposed to the common weal" null and void, and the decisions of the Courts have settled that all combinations, either of masters or workmen, with the view of controlling the labour-market, are in restraint of trade, and "opposed to the common weal." For this reason, the Court refused to grant the Unions the privileges which they thought they already possessed. The result is that, though they have ceased since 1824 to be illegal associations, they still remain unrecognized by law.*

These restrictions, which irritate without disabling, have helped to keep up the ancient feeling of enmity on the part of the workmen towards the masters; time and amendments of the law can alone remove this: nor must it be forgotten that the impartiality of the bench and public opinion act as two powerful correctives to them.

For forty-eight years the English workman has enjoyed the right of disposing of his labour as freely as the merchant disposes of his goods, or the manufacturer of his produce. The army of workmen now enrolled under the flag of Trades' Unions may vie with those of the most powerful States on the Continent: it numbers more than 800,000 volunteers. No one

* The position of Trades' Unions is somewhat improved by a temporary Act passed in 1868, defining in what respects their rules are to be regarded as acting in restraint of trade, and confining this to the regulations which compel members to conduct their labour only in a certain mode, as for instance, by the day, or the obligation to leave off work after a certain number of hours. This new law, though insufficient, is nevertheless an important security to the unions, and enabled one of them, on the 19th of December, 1868, to obtain the conviction of a dishonest treasurer.—*Author's Note.*

even among its ill-wishers can hope to scatter it: to do that it would be necessary to go back to the old tyrannical laws which sanctioned the serfdom of the working-classes. With a force so numerous and so well organized it is necessary to come to terms, the interests of all classes are concerned in persuading it to lay down its arms, and in showing it that it may find a much better use for its power than the fruitless struggles in which it has been hitherto engaged.

France cannot remain indifferent to this spectacle, nor ought she merely to seek to make a temporary profit out of the disturbed conditions of industry which these contests may cause among our neighbours; for what nation can be sure of escaping them? England will perhaps see her sails swelled by a favourable breeze, while around us the tempest is raging. In fact, the advance of wages, whatever may be the means used to obtain it, is the object of the working-classes equally in all countries; and as long as their labour is bought as a mere commodity, and not admitted to share in trade profits, it is natural that they should think only of increasing its value in the market, without caring for what may be the ulterior effects of such increase. As soon as the Legislature released the working-classes from the unjust fetters which hindered them from the free use of their labour, a strike first presented itself as the instrument whereby to defend their interests;

to keep up a strike a fund must be raised for the support of men out of work, and between this and an Union there is only the difference between a provisional institution and a permanent system.

Mr. Hewitt, an American ironmaster, and, like most of his countrymen, neither the slave of routine nor wedded to arbitrary theories, states in his evidence that "the uneasiness which exists among the labouring-men all over the world, and especially among those who are more enlightened, arises from two causes: one of these is the general introduction of machinery, by which production has been enormously increased, without (as the people believe) a corresponding re-arrangement of the laws of distribution of the proceeds. It is a feeling arising out of the belief that the profits of industry are not distributed fairly. That is the first cause. Secondly, the large introduction of gold from California and Australia has disturbed the relations of value, and labour, among other commodities, has had its value disturbed. It is reaching an adjustment, which it would reach without the Trades' Unions, but which these working-men believe they will reach more readily by the Trades' Unions." They know that international relations and intercourse are so frequent and easy that they can never hope to obtain on this account any lasting advantages, which would not, in a short time, be shared by the labouring-classes of other countries:

and when the English manufacturers reproach their workmen with exacting an increase of wages, favourable to foreign competition, the latter retort that the workmen on the Continent will in their turn soon get a rise, and that, if need be, they will help them to it; and so it will be all fair again.

The importance, then, of Trades' Unions must be evident to every one. We propose, first, to give a sketch of their general characteristics; and then to point out, adopting the same order as the Commission, that which gives them peculiar features in each trade. With this view we shall describe the part they played in Trade disputes. Lastly, we shall endeavour to discover, with the aid of some recent examples, how they may be either disarmed or what can be found to take their place, or, which would be best of all, in what way they may be employed in doing good service to society at large.

CHAPTER III.

THE ORGANIZATION OF TRADES' UNIONS.

TRADES' UNIONS are, above all things, a bank for the relief of men out of work.

As a general rule there is an entrance fee, sometimes rather high; afterwards the members pay a subscription varying from a penny to one, or in some cases as much as two, shillings a week. A reserve fund is thus created, which increases rapidly in prosperous years, and which is designed to support the members of the association when they are out of work, either from want of employment, or in consequence of a strike. The subscription is the same for all members,* and this equality is a groundwork of the institution, since it implies the equal right of all the members to support when out of work: during a strike it matters not whether a man's earnings had been large or small, whether he is a skilful or unskilful

---

* Except in the case of two or three societies, which have two scales, and in the London Printers' Union, in which alone the subscriptions are graduated according to the wages of each individual member.—*Author's Note.*

workman, the Union must keep him from starving. The amount of relief secured to him by the Union depends solely, if he is married, on the number of mouths he has to feed.

This relief naturally varies a good deal according to the trade and the resources of each society. It has more than once happened, in the course of a prolonged strike, that a Union, seeing its funds melting away, has been obliged to diminish the allowances of the members, till at last its resources have been completely exhausted. It is, therefore, the duty of the leaders of the different Unions never to engage in a struggle with the masters without having first deliberately weighed the chances.

The society is managed by a superintending or executive council, annually elected by ballot by all the members, and including a president, a treasurer, and a secretary. The government of the society, all intercourse with the masters, decisions as to strikes, the allowance of relief, together with the admission and the expulsion of members, all belong exclusively to the council. A general meeting is held for the discussion of grand financial affairs, such as the question of imposing an extraordinary subscription, called a levy, on all members, in cases where there has been a branch strike, and the normal resources of the society are insufficient to support it.

But the more important Unions, such as the

Amalgamated Engineers, the Amalgamated Society of Carpenters and Joiners, the Masons, the two great Societies of Ironworkers of Staffordshire and the North of England, the Society of Ironfounders, the Lancashire Spinners, the National Association of Miners, which numbers over 35,000 members, and many others besides, have a more complicated organization, and are each divided into a great number of branches. Each branch or lodge, which is composed of the workmen inhabiting the same district, elects its own committee, and has its special fund, of which it has the entire management, but for which it has to account every year to the central council. The central council is composed of delegates elected for six months by the different branches, in proportion to the number of members in each branch, and also of two officers, a secretary and a treasurer, appointed directly by the whole body of members.*

It is the business of the branches to admit candidates, who must first be proposed by two members; they also have to decide, in the first instance, upon rejections, relief, and local strikes. But the central authority may always be appealed to against their decisions; and if any branch were to go on strike without having obtained this authority's sanction, it would not be supported by the

* In some Unions no general executive power is elected, but the committee of each branch takes it in turn to act in that capacity.— *Author's Note.*

Union. Lastly, voting levies and hearing appeals from branches against the decisions of their central councils, is the business of general meetings. The Amalgamated Engineers have 308 branches, of which eleven are in America; and some are composed of English workmen settled in France and in Australia; the Amalgamated Carpenters and Joiners have 190; the Masons 278, and another society of Carpenters 150. In some of these associations, as, for instance, in the two first named, the balance in the hands of each branch is at the end of every year carried to a common fund, which is then divided among all the branches according to the number of their members; by this means the expenses of the Union are assessed equally upon the whole body. Others, on the contrary, allow their branches complete independence in the disposal of their finances, subject always to the liability of contributing, if necessary, to the funds of any branch needing assistance. If a member changes his abode, he acquires the right to be admitted at the end of a year into the branch established in his new residence; a simple card supplied by the branch he has left procures him admission into the other.*

* A particular colour, red, is reserved for the cards of men who have been discharged for drunkenness or bad conduct. Accordingly, the holder of a red card, though still retaining the right of admission, is viewed with suspicion by his future companions: a blue card is reserved for members admitted within the year. The best of all is a black card.—*Author's Note.*

The expulsions, which are very numerous, (in the Amalgamated Engineers' Association they amount to one-third of the number of admissions,) are almost always the result of voluntary resignation, intimated by ceasing to subscribe. A workman changes his residence, and does not always care to become a member of another society, or sometimes he neglects even to obtain admission into another branch of the same society. It frequently happens that a man, whose means have been exhausted by a long strike, and who has lived some time upon the allowance from his Union, either cannot or will not continue his subscription, and resigns. Or sometimes the association or branch decrees the expulsion of an unworthy member, or of one who has transgressed the rules. Any man continuing to work for a master, against whom his Union had decided to strike, would of course be expelled, unless he anticipated this sentence by immediate resignation.*

The fund for the assistance of men out of work is the principal feature in the Union Budget; but a few

---

* We may here take passing notice of a society called the London Working-Men's Association, which is under the direction of Mr. Potter, and aspires to be considered the general representative of all the Trades' Unions combined. It is composed of delegates appointed by some among them. But it appears not to exercise much influence, if one may judge by the manner in which the chief leaders of the unionist movement spoke of it before the Commission. They accused it, in particular, of having encouraged strikes by holding out promises that it was not, and never could have been, able to perform.—*Author's Note.*

of them, called specially "Trade Societies," confine the employment of their revenues to the support of strikes. These are not, in general, important societies. The others offer their members certain additional advantages borrowed from the mutual benefit societies: these are—a weekly allowance in case of accident, and almost always in case of sickness also, funeral expenses to the amount of 8*l*. or 12*l*., and often half these respective sums for the burial of their wives. Some associations insure their members against the loss of their tools, and three of them secure a pension to old men and invalids.

The combination of these two aims, viz., at acting both as a strike fund and as a benefit society, has been violently attacked by the adversaries of Trades' Unions; while, on the other hand, their supporters look upon it as not only advantageous but even necessary to the existence of them. It will, therefore, be useful to consider the discussions which took place on this subject before the Commission.

The two chief charges brought against these societies (called "mixed Unions") are these:—First, that of winning over, by the advantages they hold out, many men naturally disposed to stand aloof from trade quarrels, but who are afterwards obliged to join in them against their wish for fear of losing all the benefit of their accumulated subscriptions. Secondly, that of fixing their budgets on such a scale as, in the long run, to render it impossible for them under any circumstances to meet the engagements which they have contracted with their members.

To the first charge, the Union leaders reply that very few men are attracted by the advantages offered by the benefit fund only, because in all associations in which the members are allowed to choose whether they will contribute to this fund, or limit their payments to the fund for the assistance of men out of work, the subscriptions are very few in number. They allege, moreover, that the mixed Unions offer to the public in general, to the masters themselves, and, above all, to the workmen, who are always the first to suffer from a strike, much better security for prudent management than the pure trade societies. These latter, which include all the Sheffield Cutlers' Unions, have always been notorious for their intolerance and violence.

The moment they found themselves in possession of a common fund intended for strike purposes exclusively, their natural tendency would be to seek employment for it with or without reason. In mixed Unions, on the contrary, all strike expenses are so much drawn out of the relief fund, and a man who knows that every day's idleness is causing him a loss of so much future benefit on which he counted, is much less inclined to leave off work than one who could be kept in idleness out of a special fund of which, if he did not, another would take advantage. Mixed Unions, therefore, cannot be said to employ enticements to enlist men who are not naturally disposed to join in trade quarrels; but while they offer to the frugal and prudent section of the working-classes the means of supporting a contest when inevitable, they tend greatly to diminish the number of strikes, and to encourage general moderation.

The second charge leads us to examine the financial organization of these societies. Upon this their whole future depends. They are nothing but a dangerous snare, unless they succeed in establishing in the hands of the workmen a power capable of counterbalancing that possessed by the masters in their capital. This question gave rise to a long and keen argument before the Commission, between Mr. Applegarth, Secretary of the Amalgamated Association of Carpenters and Joiners, and Mr. Tucker, the actuary of a great Life Insurance Company, who was summoned by the commissioners to give evidence on this point as an expert.

Mr. Tucker, after examining all the accounts of Mr. Applegarth's great Union, and submitting them to the rules laid down for the calculation of life insurances, tontines, and mutual benefit societies, declared that the science of numbers condemned it utterly, and that all other societies organized on the same plan were on the high road to inevitable bankruptcy, which would be the more irreparable the longer it was put off.

We will take this society as a model of the mechanism and resources of these great associations. Its members have to pay five shillings entrance-money to begin with, and a shilling a week afterwards and three-pence a quarter in addition; this brings the annual subscription up to 2*l*. 13*s*. The sums so collected are carried to a common fund for defraying the whole expenditure of the society. These may be divided into three heads, viz.—I. Mutual assistance ("benefits"). II. Trade purposes. III. General expenses.

I. Benefits are subdivided thus:

1st. Assistance in sickness—twelve shillings a week for twenty-six weeks, and after that six shillings a week as long as needed. 2nd. Superannuation—five shillings a week for those who have been over twelve years, seven shillings a week for those who have been over eighteen, and eight shillings a week for those who have been over twenty-five years members. 3rd. Funeral expenses, 3*l*. 10*s*. for those who have belonged less, 12*l*. for those who have belonged more, than six months to the society.

II. Trade expenses consist of—1st. Support of strikes sanctioned by the association. Each member while on strike receives ten shillings a week for the first twelve, and six shillings a week for the twelve following weeks.

2nd. Support of members out of work. This is fixed at fifteen shillings a week in cases where they have not been discharged for misconduct. 3rd. Insurance to their full value against the loss of tools for those who can count more than six months' membership, for those who cannot the amount recoverable under this head is limited to 5*l*. 4th. An emigration bounty of 6*l*., or more if the resources of the society will permit it. 5th. Relief in case of accidents.* 6th. Aid granted to other societies to help them in supporting strikes.

III. General expenses, which amount to a large proportion of the whole, include the fixed salary of the secretaries, attendance fees of delegates and members of the council on certificate of presence, the hire of offices and of rooms to hold meetings in, and printing numerous documents, which last forms a large item.

The expenditure under these three heads amounted in 1865 to 1,635*l*., 2,790*l*., and 2,307*l*. respectively, making a total of about 6,742*l*., omitting fractions. The receipts amounted to 10,488*l*., leaving a balance of 3,746*l*., which is paid into a reserve fund kept to meet any possible future increase of the "benefit" charges.†

* In the Society's accounts this expense appears under the second head, though it would seem to belong rather to the first.—*Author's Note.*

† In order to show the relative importance of these three divisions of expenditure, the secretary of the Union has made a calculation showing the proportion which each one of them bears to the sum total of

Rather more than half the gross income, therefore, is either spent in affording present relief, or is set aside to supply future wants under this head.

It was upon this calculation that Mr. Tucker undertook to prove the insolvency of the Society.

Relying upon the tables prepared for the calculation of annuities and life insurances, he asserts that, supposing the average age of members on admission to be thirty years, the whole amount of the weekly shilling subscriptions would hardly cover the expenditure incurred under the first head ("Benefits"): and supposing the average age on admission to be forty-five, the subscription would have to be doubled: whereas it really is only sixpence a week, because only half the revenues are devoted to the expenses under the first head. It is most unjust, he says, to oblige all members, without distinction of age, to pay the same quota. A young man, who has probably thirty years of health before

---

income, taking the figure 100 to represent that sum total. According to this calculation

> The Reserve balance will be 35·80
> The "Benefits" . . . . . 15·59
> The "Trade purposes" . . 26·61
> The "General Expenses" . 22·00
> } per 100,

and the balance, or excess of income over expenditure, placed to the reserve fund, added to the sum actually spent in "benefits," which represents the sum total spent in relief, will be in the proportion 51·49 to 100, that is to say, rather more than half the whole expenditure.—*Author's Note.*

him before he will need assistance from the Society, will have to pay ten times dearer for this assistance than one already in the decline of life when admitted, and for this reason more exposed to disease and on the brink of old age. The danger which threatens mixed unions will appear only with time. Composed at first starting of healthy strong men, their expenses in the beginning are small; their receipts are enormously in excess of their expenditure; the members who have the luck (if we may say so) to fall ill during this first period are liberally assisted. But in time the generation which founded a society grows old; some of them die, and their funeral expenses must be paid; others get sick or become infirm, and must be supported. These no longer contribute to the receipts, the reserve fund melts away, and the succeeding generation finds itself obliged to bear part of these burdens. So long as the number of members goes on increasing the enlarged receipts thereby secured will cover the additional outlay, but the radical defect becomes apparent as soon as the society has reached its normal limits. The regular subscriptions are no longer sufficient, extraordinary levies are needed to meet the wants of those who did not pay enough when they were young. To escape these fresh charges the young and active members will withdraw and seek admission into a more recent and apparently more prosperous society; but this one also, like the other, must infallibly end its career in the bankruptcy court.

Much was alleged by the advocates of Trades' Unions to rebut these gloomy anticipations. Mr. Applegarth began by pointing out various sources of income overlooked by Mr. Tucker. Among these are the sums received in fines imposed on members whose subscriptions are in arrear; 400*l.* was derived from this source in 1866; all relief is withheld from these members until they have paid up; this again represents a saving (in the same year) of 250*l.*; lastly and principally, the expulsion of all members whose subscriptions have fallen in arrear beyond a certain fixed time; more than 1,000 members were expelled for this reason in 1866, by which a gain of 2,000*l.* accrued to the Society, viz. from the benefit expenditure saved to the paid-up subscription capital, and from the entrance fees that a number of members had to pay on a second and even a third admission.

Besides all this, the sanitary influence exercised over one another by the workmen is much greater than in a mutual benefit society. Trades' Unions are engines of war as well as benefit societies, and therefore admit none but strong healthy men within their ranks: false pretexts for asking assistance would be detected at once by a man's fellow-workmen, accordingly the average of sickness is very low. Lastly, the outgoings under each head have already reached the normal proportion to income, except those of the superannuation fund.

Mr. Applegarth himself admits that this last may increase to such an extent as to cause alarm for the future, unless the difficulty is obviated either by increasing the subscription or reducing the pensions. But it must be remembered that of all the Unions, with which the Commission was concerned, only three provide superannuation pensions; consequently all the others escape the dangers pointed out by Mr. Tucker.

His arguments nevertheless, as may be supposed, caused great excitement among the advocates of Trades' Unions, and notwithstanding the dryness of the subject the discussion was continued with great spirit.

Mr. Applegarth was followed by the Secretary of the Amalgamated Engineers. Mr. Allan represents one of the most powerful Unions in England; its members are more than 30,000 in number, and in 1865 its income was 86,886*l.*, its expenditure 49,172*l.*, and its reserve fund amounted to 140,000*l.* Mr. Allan can point to the experience of sixteen years,* during which time the uninterrupted prosperity of the Association has enabled

---

* This experience, in fact, goes much further back; for the Amalgamated Association, in its present form, represents several much older societies, the whole of whose liabilities it took upon itself. This accounts for its starting saddled with superannuation pensions, notwithstanding that by the rules it is necessary to have been eighteen years a member before acquiring a right to a pension.—*Author's Note.*

it gradually to augment its scale of allowances, although the deductions for this purpose from the annual subscription of 2*l*. 12*s*. paid by each member, amounted, in 1866, only to eight shillings and threepence for the sick, three shillings and twopence for superannuation, three shillings and twopence for funeral expenses, and elevenpence-halfpenny for accidents; that is to say, fifteen shillings and twopence-farthing for the whole expenditure under the head of "Benefits." He rebuts the charge of injustice brought by Mr. Tucker against the system of uniform subscriptions, by proving that the uniformity is balanced by the varying scale of entrance fees; these are graduated according to the age of the member and the value of the pension secured, of which the amount depends upon the number of years during which the pensioner has paid his subscriptions. He asserts moreover both that the number of expulsions conduces to maintain a low average age among the members, which has not varied in the course of the last ten years, and also that the average of sickness and infirmity adopted by Mr. Tucker, on which he relies to prove that the Society must become insolvent without a capital of 679,734*l*., is greatly exaggerated.

These arguments were confirmed by the representatives of other Unions in the course of the inquiry. We shall only quote Mr. Harnott, the Secretary of a

Masons' Association, which has been in existence for thirty-three years, and consisted in 1866, of 17,762 members.* In the end a most important, because thoroughly impartial authority, came forward, and reduced Mr. Tucker's alarming predictions to their true value.

Mr. Finlaison, an officer high in the public debt department, and entrusted with much statistical work by Government, has, in a report handed in to the Commission three months after the close of the discussion upon this subject, examined and reduced to their exact value the arguments which had been advanced on both sides. As this is a question of great importance to all countries, we give, in the appendix at the end of the volume, an analysis of the calculations which he made on the budgets of the two societies selected as specimens, that of the Amalgamated Engineers and the Amalgamated Carpenters and Joiners. It will there be seen that after having weighed and calculated all the circumstances favourable to the Unions, he declares that if, omitting strike expenses, the weekly subscription was raised from one shilling to eighteenpence, they would offer all the guarantee necessary to ensure their stability.

* A peculiar feature of this Association is that members, who wish to contribute only to the fund for the relief of men out of work, pay a diminished subscription, but have no right to participate in any of the benefits secured under the second head, "Trade-purposes."—*Author's Note.*

And if the reader will follow these calculations to the end, it will be clear to him that, without renouncing a strike fund, which is the principal object of their existence, but by a slight addition (say of threepence farthing) to the amount above fixed for the weekly subscription, and an inconsiderable reduction (say of one-eighth) of the charges under the first head "benefits," the Unions will be able in the future, as heretofore, to meet their engagements to the satisfaction of the most cautious accountants.*

However this may be, the advocates of Unions rise above these calculations, and take up higher ground. An Union, they say, is not a mutal insurance office, with fixed rules, whose only duty is to receive, in order to distribute them, the contributions of persons absolutely strangers to one another; it must always be borne in mind that it is the common fund of an association of persons united by the same interests, who always reserve to themselves entire liberty of disposing of it, but never irrevocably engage themselves to employ it in any particular manner. Its first duty is to meet the expense of strikes, and of assisting men out of work; and if, thanks to larger subscriptions, its funds are sufficient to relieve the wants which sickness, accidents, old age or death may cause among its members, the degree to which it can do this must depend entirely

* See Appendix.

upon its resources at the moment. The United Engineers have gradually increased their scale of allowances; but if a large portion of their reserve fund were absorbed by a strike, they would have to reduce the scale in proportion, and no one would have any right to complain. In this way the benefit system, when restored to its proper place in the Union, acts as an elastic and supplementary spring, which, while increasing the power of the association and not diverting it from its main object, regulates without shackling its energies.

This is the part assigned by the workmen themselves to the vast societies which we have merely sketched in outline, and which they support with such unanimity and perseverance by their subscriptions. This is all they ask from the principle of association in exchange for so many sacrifices. The greatness of these sacrifices, as shown by the figures we have just quoted, is an eloquent proof of the resolution and spirit of enterprise possessed by those who made them. Such associations are clearly not the work of a few picked men; they are the work of a whole population, which every week sets aside part of its wages in order to contribute to the common cause. We shall presently see with what energy the workmen endure the cruellest hardships, when, for a more or less just cause, war is declared against the masters by strike; at such times the heat of battle keeps up their strength: but real determination and force of will is shown, when a workman, who is peaceably earning his living, is seen willing to raise a sum large in proportion to his small means, and to carry it to a fund, to which perhaps he will never need to have recourse himself, and which finds favour in his eyes only by appealing to his *esprit de corps*.

Every shilling which goes into this fund—in which millions are accumulated yearly—represents a certain amount of privation endured by a workman's family for a week. The number of workmen's families, to be sure, is large: but rents are high, and meat, bread, and coal are dear. A mechanic or joiner, who has to keep his wife and perhaps four or five children out of his wages, earns from twenty-six to thirty-six shillings a week. But such a man, in calculating his resources, ought to deduct at least one quarter from his weekly receipts to allow for occasional intervals of slackness. He cannot, therefore, reckon upon his income ever rising, according to the respective rate of his weekly wages, above 47*l.* or 70*l.* in the year: the last amount is seldom reached; even iron-workers, whose work is more severe than any, do not earn, even in good years, more than 52*l.*, and this may be taken as a very fair average of the English artisan's annual income. And yet out of this 52*l.* he manages to set aside 2*l.* 12*s.*—a sum representing more than two weeks' wages—for the benefit of his Union.

Although the advantages it offers him are both distant and uncertain, he nevertheless willingly accepts the sacrifice and regularly pays in his subscription, in order that in times to come he or his children may enjoy the advantages derived from the protection of a powerful association, together with the good interest, in the form of an advance of wages, which is not infrequently obtained from investment in the Union.

As soon as the unproductive outlay on strikes has ceased to absorb the greater part of this painfully accumulated capital, it will become a new element of property in the hands of the workmen.

CHAPTER IV.

THE BUILDING TRADE.

WE have described the organization of Trades' Unions in general. We shall proceed to show how they work in the principal trades into which the Commission examined, and in the same order.

The building trade was the first selected. This is, next to agriculture, the most important industry in England, from the number of persons—nearly 900,000 —employed in it. Twenty-six witnesses, ten employers, and sixteen workmen, were examined, and the minutes of the meetings which were taken up with hearing their evidence fill four folio volumes.

The peculiar circumstances of this trade cause the separation between employers and employed to be wider than that which prevails in any other. It has no foreign or even local competition to fear, as the bricks of which all the great towns in England are built are all made in their immediate neighbourhood; but for some years past the expansion of the railway system has, by holding out prospects of large immediate returns, given a prodigious impulse, and thereby attracted an excess of capital to the trade. Under these circumstances there was a twofold competition: first, that between the various private persons who wanted to build, but were able to draw their supply of labour only from a limited area; secondly, that between the various contractors, who were urged on by the rivalry of their ever-increasing capital. This double demand, instead of acting as a counterpoise, caused a general rise of prices; first in the value of building materials, and then in that of labour. The workmen being in great request, and free to move from place to place just as they pleased, took the opportunity of obtaining an advance of wages. But it cost them many severe contests, and more than one disaster interrupted the course of their success.

In order to support these contests a number of Unions has been formed in each one of the callings connected with the building trade, such as carpenters and joiners, house-painters, brick-makers, stone-cutters, plasterers, bricklayers, stonemasons, and day labourers. Some of these Unions have branches spread all over England; others are entirely local, and sometimes even fight one another from town to town. It is difficult to ascertain the exact number of their members; one master reckons it at ten and a half per cent of the total number of men employed in the trade, which would make it 90,000; but this estimate is strongly disputed, and probably more than one-third of the adult healthy artisans are Union men.

There are two ways in which an advance of wages,—the great object of all these associations,—may be brought about: either directly, when an employer pays a workman a higher price for a day's work, or for a particular job; or indirectly, when the number of working hours is diminished without any corresponding reduction of the day's wages. Under every shape, and in every trade, the Unions will be found always pursuing this double object. But the customs and rules which they endeavour to enforce as tending to procure these advantages vary greatly, and are sometimes based on quite opposite principles. In the building trade piecework, which is certainly more equitable in theory, and more consistent with individual liberty than work by the day, is allowed only among the painters and brickmakers; all the other branches of the trade accuse the masters of employing it only to save expense by exciting among the men a spirit of rivalry, which shall lead to the lowering of wages and the lengthening of the day's work; and accordingly they are violently opposed to it. The fact that the leading contractors are agreed on this point with their men, and prefer paying them by the day, proves that it is both difficult and dangerous to apply the piecework system to this trade. But although payment by the day is the plan generally accepted by both sides, the method of applying it is nevertheless a frequent cause of disputes. The men claim the right of subjecting it to various rules, which the masters refuse to acknowledge. Above all, they accuse the masters of engaging certain labourers with the understanding that they are indirectly to be allowed all sorts of advantages on the condition of getting over their work more speedily, so as to act as an example and incentive to the rest. These workmen are called *bell horses*, and are the special object of dislike to their companions. Some Unions, especially that of the bricklayers, are not satisfied with resisting piecework only, but attempt to limit the amount of work to be done by each man, so as to arrive at perfect uniformity of wages. The system of payment by the day does not prevent men of known skill and activity from obtaining higher wages than others: of this just advantage it is sought to deprive them by obliging them to enter into the unfair engagement not to perform each day more than a certain fixed average of work.

Other Unions, though less despotic, nevertheless fix the minimum wage which it shall be lawful for their members to accept. They say that, unless this is done, the masters take advantage of a workman's poverty to offer him a reduced salary, and then, as soon as the opportunity offers, lower their whole scale of payments accordingly. To this the masters reply that this minimum is really a maximum; and that, in order to make up for the amount paid to bad workmen above the just remuneration of their labour, they are obliged to refuse good workmen the advantages which otherwise they would have bestowed on the deserving by way of encouragement. It is easy to see that in this question the selfishness of both sides plays a more important part than their material interests; for the average of men's labour generally is so uniform that it can only be excelled by a few quite exceptional workmen, who, under any circumstances, are sure always to be able to make good terms for themselves.

Unionist workmen, always with a view to the advance of wages, attach special importance to what they call protection of trade. This expression is popular just because it is vague, and because everyone can interpret it as he pleases. Mixing views as to monopoly, worthy only of a bygone time, with some just and equitable ideas, Unionists assert, as a trade privilege, the right of limiting the number of apprentices, and of forbidding all who have not passed through a regular apprenticeship to practise their trade. In default of legal sanction they ask the Unions to intervene in support of these claims.

In most branches of the building trade a beginner

must still be bound by indentures to a master, whereby he engages to serve him, at a reduced salary, for five or six years. He pays for his instruction, which is in fact his capital, by working for his master, after he has gained experience in his craft, at this reduced rate; but the men, with whom he has worked, say then, and not without reason, that seeing they have employed part of their time in teaching him, they, and not the master, ought to be paid for it. They say " if we are to get nothing for teaching him, we have at least the right to refuse, or to limit our pupils to the number which suits us."

The artisan, late apprentice, looks upon the knowledge which he has purchased by so many years of ill-paid toil as his actual property; he considers as an intruder and a counterfeit not only any workman who has not gone through the same training as himself, but even any one who, having been apprenticed to a different branch of the trade, should attempt to join that to which he belongs, or even to encroach, in the merest trifle, on what he considers as his special department. "We do not," he says, "ask the law to extend to us the same protection as that granted to the privileges of lawyers and doctors, and the other, so-called, liberal professions; we try to obtain this by the establishment of Unions." It must be owned that this system, which, carried to extremes, would doubtless be fatal to trade, has certainly the advantage of employing no legal intervention to attain its aims.

We ought to look upon the protective rules of some of the Unions merely as the errors of a power which has not yet gained experience, and is still acting in obedience to old prejudices. Instances of this, which are happily rare, are mostly found among the brickmakers, who are notorious for their intolerance and violence, not to mention the two murders of which they were guilty at Manchester. They go by night to the yards of the masters whom they dislike, and trample upon the unbaked bricks; this they call "trotting out the blind horse;" and if they owe a grudge to one of their fellow-workmen, they fill the clay which he has to knead with needles. It is by no means surprising that they should have opposed the introduction of machinery, inasmuch as they believed that it tended to diminish their wages. But this opposition, which was mistaken under any circumstances, did not cease even when the masters offered them a share in the increased profits which these improvements were certain to realize. They looked upon machinery only as a sort of artificial arms which competed with their labour and reduced the number of men employed: they did not see that increased cheapness of production, by promoting consumption, must benefit the whole body; on the contrary, their only object was to oblige the masters to divide a job among the largest possible number of men, even if the wages of each man employed suffered from it. Next they attempted to apply a system of local protection by dividing the country into districts. Each district was to suffice to itself: the master brickmakers in each were to employ none but the men of the district, were to bake the clay in the district only, and were to sell their bricks only in the district, with the alternative of being put under ban.

The workmen, relying upon the strength of their Unions, seek to make the masters both engage to give them one, or several, weeks' previous notice of discharge, and also agree to reduce the hours of work. This reduction, as we have already explained, is only a disguised advance in wages if the day's pay remains the same; but if the pay is diminished in proportion,—if, for instance, it is fixed at so much an hour,—it becomes merely, either morally or physically, a sanitary question, but one of great importance; for it is certain that, in a great number of trades, a day's work of twelve or even of ten hours is a hurtful excess. There are mines in which it has been found necessary to fix the maximum at six or seven hours; and Parliament has had to interfere in order to limit the number of hours in factories. Provided the demand for labour, on which the workman depends for his living, is not diminished by this reduction, his cultivation and intellectual life will derive great advantage from it. Although the abandonment of the long day system has doubtless been a public benefit, the Unions never professed to forbid it utterly: all they wanted was that all extension of the hours of work should be regarded as exceptional and carry higher pay, and that any man might be allowed to refuse to work over hours without being held to have broken his agreement.

By way of enforcing their demands, the Unions can at present resort only to a strike; and, accordingly, the list of strikes in the building trade in the course of the last forty years is innumerable. But from the trade being essentially local, its disputes are generally confined to the spot in which they rose, and seldom attain to large proportions.

The disastrous ending of one of the earliest and most important of these contests was a blow from which the Unions did not for a long time recover.

In 1833, eight years after the repeal of the Combination Laws, the Unions began to make their power felt at Liverpool: at first they used it to effect considerable improvement in the position of the workmen there, but soon, as might be expected, they began to abuse their newly-acquired power. Not content with resisting them, the masters declared war against the very existence of these societies; and, in order to fight them, established a combination of their own, and entered into a mutual engagement to employ no man who would not solemnly forswear the Union. This at once shut the door to all compromise, and touched the English workman in the most sensitive part, his spirit of independence; accordingly, these terms were unanimously rejected. The masters thereupon closed their establishments by way of anti-strike; this is called in trade language a "lock-out." The workmen held out, so all business came to a standtill, and a state of general prosperity was succeeded by ruin among the masters, and a state of frightful misery among the men. The consumption of bricks, in the town of Liverpool alone, fell at once from one million a week to twenty thousand. The contractors had men fetched from other parts of England; but the Unions placed pickets around their establishments, who exhorted the newcomers not to go in, took them back to the railway station, and paid their fares home. They succeeded thus in preventing the masters from resuming business, but not in enabling their members to resume work without signing the act of repudiation, which was the origin of the quarrel. The support, which they had sought beyond Lancashire, soon failed them. A meeting of delegates from all the Trades' Associations, representing more than 30,000 persons, was held at Manchester to uphold their cause, but it separated after having spent a great deal of money and done very little. Nevertheless, as long as they had a penny left, they would not own they were beaten. At length, after more than six months of extreme poverty, they were obliged to yield. The stoppage of their wages during this period was a loss to the workmen of more than 72,000*l*; and, in addition to this, they had to pay nearly 18,000*l*. for Union expenses. The Unions were relinquished for the moment, but they were sure to be re-established on the first opportunity.

They re-appeared first in London. Ever since the year 1847, the workmen in the capital had been simultaneously pursuing the two objects of obtaining a direct advance in wages, and a reduction of the hours of labour; but their demands having been always complied with, the influence of the Unions was not apparent. The day's wage had been raised successively from five shillings, to five and sixpence, and then to six shillings; besides this, it had been settled that on Saturdays, though paid as for a whole day, they should leave off work at four o'clock; this was subsequently extended to one o'clock. But the workmen had till then in vain requested that the ordinary day's work might be reduced from ten hours to nine. At last, in 1859, the various Unions combined together under the guidance of the London Working Men's Association and its Secretary, Mr. Potter, and resolved to obtain this fresh concession; nor did they make any secret of their intention, as soon as they had gained this point, of renewing their efforts until the day's work was limited to eight hours, without any corresponding reduction in wages.*

A great many members of them happened at that time to be out of work; and they believed that, by reducing the day's work from ten hours to nine, ten men would be required instead of nine to get through the same work, and that consequently the hands standing idle would have a better chance of obtaining employment. Their calculation would have been right if they would have consented that exactly the same amount of remuneration should be divided among ten as was before received by the nine. But, in order to enable the Unions to saddle, as they wanted, the employer with the expense of the tenth man, the state of the trade ought to have been such as to warrant their being exacting in their demands, and such as to make it more advantageous for the contractors to accept fresh sacrifices than to face a strike. They ought to have understood that the slackness of work, which they wanted to remedy, was the consequence of a

* This limit has been adopted in Australia, where labour, owing to its scarcity, is able to lay down the law. It is also very much in use in the United States, in which it has been the subject of sharp discussion. Several States—New York among others—have recognized eight hours as the legal day's work,—as that which is to be always understood in contracts, unless the contrary is specified; and the eight hours' system has been recently introduced in the Federal arsenals. But the workmen have not found in it the advantage which they expected; for, by an inevitable reaction in the market, the masters have reduced rateably their payments for the days so curtailed, and the Federal Government set the first example for taking this step.—*Author's Note.*

stagnation of business, which rendered compliance with their demands impossible. There being no chance, under these circumstances, of an increased demand, the masters would, naturally, prefer even a total cessation of business to an increase of expenditure.

The men concentrated all their attacks upon the great firm of the Messrs. Trollope; the workmen employed by them struck for nine hours as the day's work, while the men in the other contractors' firms went on working ten hours, and subscribed to pay those on strike. They expected to get the better of the Messrs. Trollope, and after that to bring the other firms to terms. The struggle began on July 23, 1859, preceded by tedious negotiations carried on between Mr. Potter and some employers, who represented a society composed of about seventy London firms, which, although established for twenty-five years, had never before been concerned in any dispute about wages. These firms, that of the Messrs. Trollope among them, having decided to resist, had in the month of April previously called a meeting of all the contractors to ask for their support. This meeting resulted in the establishment of a powerful combination, which soon set to work under the name of The Master Builders' Central Association. The Messrs. Trollope having failed, after the lapse of a fortnight, to supply the place of the workmen who had left them, the association declared a lock-out, whereupon all the master builders discharged their men, to the number of 7,856. They not only proclaimed that this harsh measure would be persevered in as long as the strike against the Messrs. Trollope lasted, but they decided, like the masters at Manchester, that henceforth they would employ only men entirely unconnected with any Union. A declaration containing a formal abjuration of these societies was posted up in their workshops, and every man who came in search of employment had to sign it. After a time the Messrs. Trollope succeeded in obtaining four hundred old or fresh workmen, whereupon the other masters removed the lock-out; but they continued to exact renunciation of the Union. The workmen on strike, in spite of their distress, refused to submit to this condition, and the strike was prolonged until at last mutual tacit concessions put an end to it. The workmen relinquished their demand for the extra hour, and returned in a body to the Messrs. Trollope; the masters ceased to exact any conditions opposed to the Unions. This contest, therefore, was entirely without results to either side; the workmen did not succeed in establishing nine hours as the day's work, and the masters could not break up the Unions; but, happily, in spite of the passions it raised, it was unaccompanied by any acts of violence. The London workmen have been long trained in the practice of association and combination; they are better educated than their country brethren, and anxious to set the latter a good example in all things; accordingly, their conduct on this occasion was marked by a moderation which excited the admiration even of their opponents.

There was a temporary lull: the workmen closed up their ranks, while the masters began soon to be divided by competition. In 1861 the nine hours' controversy was renewed, but this time with more skill and discretion on the part of the masters. Instead of resisting point-blank the demands made upon them, they offered the workmen a slight increase of wages, and substitution of payment by the hour for payment by the day. Up to this time, the question of what ought to be the length of a day's work had never been considered with reference to the amount of a day's pay. These two distinct questions, hitherto confounded, were separated in this fair proposal, which was accepted, and has since worked to the satisfaction of both sides. Since this time the day's pay has depended upon the number of hours of which the day consists; and the price by the hour, which was fixed in 1861 at sevenpence, was, without a struggle, raised to sevenpence halfpenny in 1865, and to eightpence in 1866.

The example set by London was not universally followed. The importance of the object aimed at may be held to have justified a strike on that occasion; but the one which broke out at Manchester in April, 1864, shows that often the more trivial the cause for these struggles the more disastrous they are in their effects; for, when men are blinded by selfishness to their true interests, obstinacy prevails over reason. The Corporation of Manchester were building assize courts; now a large and fine edifice, which somewhat relieves the monotony of the smoky city. A foreman named Kettle, who was already unpopular as a stranger in the town, placed a new comer, whom he brought with him, at the head of the journeymen. Usage required that the new comer should rank last, the old hands alone having a right to regular employment. The journeymen protested, and the committee of their Union having in vain applied to Mr. Kettle, they demanded the discharge of this man, first from the contractor, then from the architect; on this being refused, they struck work. The bricklayers, whose work had been interrupted by this dispute, maintained that Mr. Kettle was the cause of it, and demanded 25*l*. as damages, not getting which, they too went on strike. The struggle then raged with a fierceness which was revived, even in the presence of the Commission, whenever any of the principal actors in it, such as Mr. Kettle, had to give an account of its doings. Men were fetched from London to take the place of those who refused to work, but the London Bricklayers' Association interfered to prevent this, and paid their travelling expenses back. Mr. Kettle searched all England for labourers; everywhere he was met by the Manchester Union, resolved, at any price, to carry them off from him. Pickets were posted; both entreaties and threats were used to the new comers. Mr. Kettle installed them in some unfinished buildings, where he lodged and fed them, and had them guarded by policemen; but it was in vain: the seduction employed prevailed, and very few resisted the bribe of 5*l*., or, in some cases, 7*l*. 10*s*., which the Union offered them for going away. All the works which the contractor, who had insisted on keeping Mr. Kettle, had in hand were declared under strike. At last, when the bricklayers perceived that, in spite of all their efforts, the masonry of the building would be finished, they bribed the joiners to join in the strike; but in vain,—the assize courts were completed without them, and in spite of them.

The Manchester Bricklayers' Union spent 920*l*. in this unhappy contest; its own committee, which was for this year invested with the executive control of the whole association (of which the Manchester Union is only a branch), drew this sum out of the general treasury. The committee was severely blamed for this violation of rules; but, subsequently, their proceeding was sanctioned by the vote of a general meeting, which alone can authorize any disposal of the common fund of the Society.

This story shows to what extremes on both sides quarrels founded on a purely personal question may lead. After a strike has once begun, unanimity among the workmen is the first condition of success. If some of them go on working for an employer whom others want to lay under an interdict, the privations to which the latter submit are perfectly useless. They must, therefore, obtain not only the co-operation of the disciplined host of Unionists, but also the connivance of their non-Unionist brethren. They often, as we have seen, have to pay an enormous price for this connivance. If they cannot obtain it, it comes very quickly to a quarrel between them. This subject is constantly cropping up in the examinations before the Commission. All the masters and all the workmen have each their word to say, their story to tell, either in accusation or in exculpation of the Unions.

Among the former, Mr. Mault, secretary of an employers' association at Birmingham, attacked the Unions in a clever and spirited speech. He brought forward against them a good many objectionable practices, and some even guilty acts; but he seems to us to be too much given to draw general conclusions from solitary instances; and that he holds the Unions responsible for many opinions which have been professed, and for many deeds which have been committed, in places where these societies have never existed.

The two principal charges brought against them are, first, that they render strikes more frequent, and lengthen their duration; secondly, that they exercise a threefold tyranny, viz., over non-Unionists, over Unionists themselves, and over masters.

In answer to the first, the advocates of Unions have no difficulty in proving that strikes occur as frequently in districts where these societies are unknown as in those in which they are accused of fomenting them. They maintain that if they do sometimes lengthen their duration, on the other hand they often prevent them from breaking out. Mr. Williams, secretary of the National Association of Plasterers, a very large and important society, cites the case of a strike at Aberystwith, in Wales. On this occasion, the plasterers employed in the erection of two hotels took advantage of the pressing nature of the work, and suddenly demanded an advance in wages and a reduction of hours. The contractor appealed to Mr. Williams, and the Union, considering that the workmen were in the wrong, not only refused to uphold them, but provided him with others to supply the place of the deserters. Mr. Williams laid before the Commission a letter, in which a contractor expresses his gratitude to Unions, and declares that they are of the utmost service to the trade. A master at Scarborough, short of labourers, also applied to him : so that here we have the Union performing the part of labour-purveyors. Other examples might be adduced to prove that the executive councils of the large Unions have often interfered to stop the strikes of their local branches.

To the second charge, that of being a despotic minority, which, by its disciplined strength, imposes its will upon a majority indifferent to its aims and un-affected by its interests, the Unionists answer that— First, their number is much more considerable than is generally believed, and that in several branches of the building trade they form, not a minority, but an immense majority; that they include among their members all the most active and most industrious men in each trade; and finally, that you must not believe in the alleged hostility or even indifference of non-Unionists toward Unionists. Although not members of the Association and subscribers to its funds, they have the same aspirations, the same wants as their brethren in the Union, and wish them most heartily success in all their undertakings; for they are well aware that they will themselves profit indirectly by any success obtained by the Union, and in any question of wages they almost invariably make common cause with it. The reason why non-Unionists are not admitted in workshops where Unionists form a large majority, is, that inasmuch as the association has been the means of raising the wages paid in these establishments, it is not fair that those who have borne no share in its burdens should profit by its efforts. With the exception of the unfortunate occurrences at Manchester and Sheffield, none but perfectly lawful measures have been employed to enforce this exclusion. "If the masters are to be free to choose their workmen, if the men are to be free to stand aloof from our association," they say, "we Unionists too have the right to be free to leave both masters and men alone together, if the goings-on in any workshop do not happen to suit us."

On the other hand, their opponents allege that these demands and this exclusiveness, though founded on the exercise of an indisputable right, may sometimes be carried so far as to justify the application of the old maxim, "Summum jus summa injuria." There are instances of the works of some masters having been deserted (Mr. Howroyd's at Bradford, Mr. Dixon's at Blackpool,) because they employed their own sons, who did not become members of the Union; or because the number of apprentices allowed in the workshops was too large. Lastly, there is a certain class of workmen frequently alluded to in the Commission, with whom the Union is always in a state of open war. These men, called "Blacks," are in the habit of taking advantage of a strike to obtain, as long as it lasts, high wages, with the intention of going away and seeking employment elsewhere, as soon as, on the termination of the struggle,—by the victory or defeat, as the case may be, of the Union,—the establishment in which they have been working is open again to the members of it. In certain trades, and in certain districts, among the brickmakers in Lancashire for instance, these men are exposed to every conceivable outrage. Some Unions cause a regular proscribed list, in which their names are inserted, to be drawn up, this is called "the black list." Whoever figures in this list is under ban, all Unionists are forbidden to work with him.* In this list are found the names of workmen who have refused to join in a strike, who have quarrelled with the Union for any other reason, or who have broken some rule, and sometimes even of those whose evidence in court has led to the conviction of a companion accused of having carried his zeal for the Union beyond lawful limits. One society of masons is said to have a black list of more than 2,500 names, some of which have been kept on it since 1841. The passions aroused by long and painful struggles may account for, but cannot justify these practices. The leading advocates of Unions even, while alleging that the men thus put under ban are generally in themselves unworthy of interest, seek only to prove that these cases are rare, and not infrequently provoked by the conduct of the masters. Allowing, they say, that these may

* Sometimes, when for any reason the Unionists are afraid of proceeding to this extremity, the prohibition is confined to forbidding all intercourse by word of mouth with the object of their dislike. They call this "sending a man to Coventry." Men have been known to go on working for weeks with companions who would not give them a word in answer to any sort of question.—*Author's Note.*

be the habits of some local branches, still the large societies, instead of approving of them, conduce to the prevalence of a less intolerant spirit.

Another complaint frequently brought against the Unions is, the oppression which they are said to exercise over their own members. In proof of this the fines are mentioned which they impose for breaking the rules, or even for offending against mere customs, which are condemned by common sense, and sanctioned only by tradition. Such is the custom which forbids a workman to carry more than a certain number of bricks at one load. But it was proved before the Commission that, although some societies allowed these inexcusable attempts at coercion, a great many other Unions never employed the formidable power of inflicting fines except for the moral improvement of the workmen, by punishing drunkards and bad characters. Lastly, the Unions are accused of being as tyrannical to the masters as they are to the men. The behaviour of the brickmakers at Manchester was mentioned as one among many examples of this. These men will not allow machinery to be used, and obtained a promise from the masons that the latter should go on strike whenever a contractor wanted to use other than hand-made bricks; the same promise was made to the stonecutters, who also feared that certain machines might compete with their labour. It is doubtless true that the Unions have often employed their influence in fettering free action on the part of the masters, whenever, whether rightly or wrongly, they believed that in so doing they were serving the interests of labour. Can it be expected that men, embittered by suffering and struggling, should not now and then abuse a new power created by their hands? Because a tree needs pruning, should it be accused of bearing only sour fruit, and therefore cut down? Is there any human institution of which the rise is not marked with arbitrary acts? Fortunate and rare indeed is the one which has not, at any period of its existence, sought the protection of unjust and oppressive laws.

It is not, however, the workmen only who have gone beyond the bounds of moderation in these contests. Certain masters' associations have borrowed from the Unions some of the practices for which the latter are most blamed. Some of them, too, as well as some of the workmen's societies, keep their black list, and forbid any of their members to give employment to the man whom they have proscribed by inserting his name in it. Numerous witnesses can prove that leaders of strikes thus marked have gone about from door to door soliciting work in vain, and been rejected on all sides as dangerous enemies.*

* Most of the masters, however, look upon these harsh measures simply as fair retaliation; but some among them condemn them severely, and have always refused to join in them.—*Author's Note.*

Sometimes, too, the influence exercised by these combinations of masters on the rate of wages is quite as adverse to liberty of contract as the most protective rules of the working men's associations; as, for instance, in cases where they have made all their members enter into a mutual engagement that not one of them shall make any advance in favour of the workmen in his employ without the joint consent of all.

It is noteworthy, in the midst of these mutual accusations, that, whenever the raising of wages is discussed, the two sides seem to have changed parts. An advance is the avowed aim of the Unions; but, instead of blaming them for this, the masters endeavour to prove that the efforts of the men have not contributed to it, and that the ordinary course of business would have secured the same advantages to them without the heavy costs to which they have been put by their interference with it. The men, on the contrary, maintain that, without the efforts of their associations, the remuneration of labour would be lower than it is now; and that, consequently, they are answerable for the increased expenses imposed on contractors. Examples may certainly be adduced which confirm the masters' assertion. We will mention one, taken from the evidence of an impartial and experienced man, Mr. Rupert Kettle. A strike occurred at Wolverhampton, just at the time when the Government was having vast fortifications built at Portsmouth. The Union sent the workmen, who were standing idle at Wolverhampton, to Portsmouth, where they easily found employment. But the competition caused by their arrival prevented wages from rising at Portsmouth; while, at the same time, the masters whom they had quitted, being ruined by the stoppage of the works, which they had taken under contract, could make no concession in order to put an end to the strike, and preferred enduring it to submitting to the demands of their workmen. Now, but for the interference of the Union, a competition would naturally have arisen between the Government on the one hand, in haste to get the forts finished, and the masters on the other, not only at Wolverhampton, but in all the great towns in England, who would all have been afraid of losing their workmen and failing in their contracts. This competition must have raised the value of labour. But it will not do to draw general conclusions from this solitary case.

A Trades' Union is a two-edged weapon, which at first it seems easy to handle, but which is sure to wound anyone who uses it awkwardly. Every time they have tried directly to violate the laws which rule the balance of trade, they have failed signally. They have never been able to produce a fictitious rise in wages when the market was falling; but their weight in the scale is one that in these days cannot be disregarded. Under favourable circumstances they may hasten a rise and carry it to a figure that it would not otherwise have reached; and when, in consequence of the stagnation of business, the value of labour is falling, they may retard and diminish its depreciation. An unanswerable proof of this influence was brought before the Commission; viz., that in the same trade, in the same town, and with workmen of equal ability, it often happens that the wages of the Unionists are very much higher than those obtained by non-Unionists.

In no spirit of barren criticism, but in order to show the dangers which both masters and workmen have to avoid, we have sought out what foundation there was for the mutual charges which they bring against each other. We shall not have to return to this subject in detail, for the abuses, the errors, and the violence, which it has been our duty to point out in speaking of the building trade, are happily of rarer occurrence in the industries which we are about to examine.

CHAPTER V.

THE IRON TRADE.

EVERYONE knows that the iron trade is one of the principal sources of the power and prosperity of England. The various qualities of the metal, the abundance of coal in the districts where it is found, the facility of communication—everything, in short, favours this great industry. Those who have travelled by night between Birmingham and Liverpool will, doubtless, remember passing through a vast district, which seems completely to realise one of the circles of "Dante's Inferno." All is fire and smoke; on every side tower high furnaces surmounted with crests of flame which the wind twists and shakes as if it was trying in vain to tear them from their base. Through the lurid glare, which they shed around, the great arms of the lifting and pumping engines are seen tossing about like creatures in torment; while engines, panting as if breathless from the weight behind them, slowly drag trains of trucks laden with iron-ore along the tramways that cross and recross each other in every direction. The surface of the earth, deprived of all vegetation, is covered with heaps of refuse from the furnaces, called slags, which from their regular shape resemble the shells of some species of gigantic antediluvian oyster. In some places they lie soaking in pools of inky water; in others, when fresh from the furnace, they are still red like lava in a state of fusion. This is the "Black Country," which has Wolverhampton for its capital, and extends over the greater part of Staffordshire and the adjacent districts. A large and industrious population works the rich iron mines of this country. A more valuable property than these mines does not exist in all England. The Staffordshire iron is exported to all parts of the world, and is rivalled only by that from Belgium. They are, for the most part, in the hands of joint stock companies; but some of them belong to great landed proprietors, of whom Lord Dudley is one. This district is generally divided into North and South Staffordshire.

The other mineral districts of Great Britain are: in the centre of England, South Yorkshire, of which Leeds is the head-quarters; in the north, large portions of Cumberland, with the districts of Cleveland, Gateshead, and the banks of the Tyne; in Scotland, Lanarkshire; and in Wales, the north coast of the Bristol Channel.

The iron is manufactured on the spot. Many of the

owners of mines have attached to them a coal-pit, furnaces, a forge, and a limestone quarry,* so as to unite in one establishment all the chief requirements of the process. Likewise in all the great towns in these districts, such as Liverpool, Manchester, Birmingham, Wolverhampton, Leeds, Newcastle and Glasgow, vast iron works are erected, in which the pig-iron produced in the neighbourhood or in other districts is worked, sometimes into wrought-iron, sometimes into steel, and afterwards into every shape that the metal is capable of taking. Thousands of workmen are engaged in transforming the metal, glowing with heat and light, in these magnificent establishments. They are the grand monuments of modern civilization, which, if prosaic, is at the same time laborious, intelligent, patient and powerful. The workmen are divided into trades, or rather various branches of the whole Industry, according to the different processes in which they are employed. The pig-iron needs to be cleansed from all extraneous matter, and particularly from the silica and coal, which it brought out with it on leaving the blast furnace. It is melted again in a puddling furnace. A workman stirs the melted metal with a long iron bar in order to hasten the combustion of

* In blast furnaces, a certain proportion of limestone is added to the mixture of coal and ore, in order to purify the crude or pig-iron.— *Author's Note.*

the coal and the separation of the silicates; gradually the iron attaches itself to the bar and thickens, forming in the middle of the now liquid impurities a round mass, which is then withdrawn from the furnace to be placed under the steam-hammer. The repeated blows of this hammer squeeze out the slag still remaining in the dilated pores of the metal. Lastly, if it is intended to make slabs, rail-blooms, or simple bars of wrought-iron, the mass, first heated red hot, is rolled between two rolls brought gradually nearer and nearer together. Hence, the artisans are divided into three classes, the puddlers, the hammermen, and the rollers; they all begin by being apprentices, who in this trade join the artisans at work, and are necessary to them by way of assistants. To these must be added a fourth class, that of the labourers, to whom is left the execution of work needing only muscular strength. On penetrating, for the first time, into this hive, where so many strong and intelligent men are subduing both iron and fire by using each against the other, and are working together with such regularity, a stranger is struck only with the triumphs of science and industry. But if he then seeks to discover by what passions, what interests, what hopes all these men, united in a common work, are animated, he will meet with nothing but obscurity. The masters will tell him little, the workmen less. The Commission has the great merit of having made them speak before the whole world, and of having placed them face to face before the eyes of the public. Its fifth volume is devoted to this subject.

At the first glance the peculiar characteristics of this industry may be distinguished, and it is evident that it is composed of a class of workmen, in whom intelligence and a spirit of enterprise have been developed by high wages and piecework. Among them, the first place belongs to the puddlers, because their duties at the furnace enable them to lay down the law; they prepare the metal which subsequently passes through the hands of the hammermen, the rollers, and the labourers, consequently all these branches are thrown out of work if the puddlers go on strike. Accordingly the representatives of the puddlers and some of the principal iron-masters took the leading part in the discussion before the Commission. This discussion, in which the two powers were brought face to face, is more comprehensive and exhaustive than any we have hitherto followed. It will be found that workmen are inclined to be moderate in their conduct and reasonable in their demands in proportion as they are conscious of the strength of the association in which they are united; accordingly, as might be expected, the crimes, which have sometimes disgraced other trades, are unknown in the history of the iron-workers. 'In discussing the wages question, they showed that they are well acquainted with all the important questions relating to their trade, and that they observe attentively all the circumstances which can exercise any influence over it. This industry, which supplies the whole world, is, on that very account, essentially variable, and the labour, which is its principal expense, is paid in proportion to the value of its produce; it follows, therefore, that the wages in it must constantly vary, and that the workmen are just as much interested as the owners in taking account of all the fluctuations in the price of iron.*

We find no more discussions on the relative merits

---

* The Commission attempted to ascertain the portion which ought to be put down to wages, out of the total expenditure of an iron factory. The ironmasters gave no effectual assistance in this, doubtless because they were afraid of giving the heads of a calculation which would have afforded a clue to their financial situation. Those who were asked, reckoned this portion at four-fifths, or nine-tenths of the expenses of a factory, where the coal-pit, the iron mine, the limestone quarry, the furnaces, and the forge are all in the same hands; at two-thirds for one where the pigs have to be bought. But in these figures they included all the fixed salaries of the clerks, book-keepers, porters, &c., as well as the varying wages of the workmen. Besides, they justly remarked that the proportion of wages to total expenditure varies according to production. There are certain fixed and regular expenses, viz :—the royalty or permanent rent paid on the mine, the fixed salaries, and the interest of the capital invested in the undertaking. The profits on one side, the wages on the other, are, therefore, alone directly affected by production, which again regulates the annual sum spent in labour; and the admixture of fixed with variable elements in a value that is itself variable, is constantly changing the proportion which each bears to the other.—*Author's Note.*

of piecework and work by the day. The latter system of labour, upon which other trades lay such stress, is, among iron-workers, reserved for mere labourers, and considered degrading to an artisan.

The puddlers, hammermen, and rollers are paid so much for every ton of iron puddled, hammered, or rolled. The rate of this wage by the ton is itself regulated according to the value of iron by means of a sliding-scale, which was introduced in 1847 by Mr. Thorneycroft, an iron-master, and was soon after adopted throughout almost all England. According to this system the puddlers get five per cent. and the other artisans ten per cent. on every increase in the price of iron, and when the market falls, their wages are reduced in the same proportion. If, for instance, the value of a ton increases by one pound, the puddler will get one shilling extra for every ton of iron puddled; the hammerman will get two shillings extra for every ton hammered; and the roller also two shillings for every ton that passes through the rolling mill.

In Staffordshire the masters of the mining district meet every quarter to fix the price of the iron produced by the various works in the district: this, when settled, is published in a printed list, which is taken as the official scale on which wages are to be regulated; but the fluctuations in the price of iron do not always allow sales to be made at the prices so fixed. Most of the

Iron works are unable to command them; and only certain qualities of iron of rare excellence, and stamped with the most valued trade-marks, have ever been known to go beyond them.

In the north of England, where the sliding-scale is also adopted, each master is, to a great extent, free to fix his own prices, and, consequently, also the rate of the wages he pays; in Wales, on the contrary, wages are very little affected by the fluctuations of the market.*

The sliding-scale system, though tending to diminish the disputes arising out of the wages question, does not entirely prevent them. Its starting-point may be, and in fact has been, several times modified. Mr. Thorneycroft settled that the puddlers should receive exactly five per cent., or one-twentieth, on the market price of iron; subsequently the latter succeeded in

* This peculiarity is not at all surprising in a country so different from England,—different in language, in traditions, in character, in manners, in religion, and in political opinions. Its population, of Celtic origin, and almost republican in feeling, is active and laborious; but, at the same time, turbulent and fickle. The form which association assumes among the Welsh, offers another instance of their dissimilarity from the Anglo-Saxon race. They are almost all Dissenters, and opposition to the Established Church has caused a large development of *religious* association among them; they devote large sums to the support of their own forms of worship, which, as is the case with the Catholics in Ireland, depend entirely upon voluntary contributions; but the Welsh miners, and their number is large, have never taken kindly to Trades' Unions. The only Welsh Union mentioned before the Commission was dissolved a short time after its establishment, in consequence of the treasurer making off with the strong box. –*Author's Note.*

establishing that,—without altering this percentage of increase or reduction, as the case might be, in their pay, in addition to it,—they should be paid a fixed sum of sixpence, afterwards raised to one shilling per ton puddled. In this way a ton of iron sold for 8*l*., by which originally they would have gained eight shillings, would be worth to them eight shillings and sixpence and nine shillings respectively. If its value fell from 8*l*. to 7*l*., their pay, suffering a proportionate reduction, would fall to seven and sixpence and eight shillings; but when it rose to 9*l*., they would get nine and sixpence and ten shillings on it. There were some difficulties, however, in carrying out this system. Suppose two lumps of iron weighing a ton each, and exactly alike, to have been turned out by two puddlers, and that one of them, after being hammered, fetches 8*l*., and the other, in consequence of having gone through the process of rolling after the hammering, reaches the increased value of 8*l*. 10*s*., on which of these two prices ought the pay of the two puddlers, which evidently ought to be equal, to be calculated? The rate of this pay does not always immediately follow the fluctuations in the price of iron, as it ought to do according to the principle of the sliding-scale; and, lastly, the working of this scale has been disturbed by some recent improvements in machinery. Immense steam-hammers of more than twenty-five tons power, which shake the whole neighbourhood at each blow, have been established in Sir John Brown's works at Sheffield, in the Mersey Iron Works, at Mr. Krupp's works at Essen, and in some of the large factories in France. The manufacture of armour-plates has also led to the construction of rolling mills of immense power. Owing to these machines, which do not require more men to work them, the same quantity of iron can be hammered or rolled in a much shorter time than formerly, while no progress has been made in the puddlers' department, who continue stirring the liquid metal exposed to the burning heat of the furnace, without being able, in the course of their day, to puddle a greater weight than they could twenty years ago. Great inequality therefore must prevail, if the amount of wage payable to all the workmen is to remain fixed according to the same tariff. A few years ago, owing to a new hammer introduced at the Mersey Iron Works, two men, who worked no harder than their companions, made, one of them 400*l*., the other 450*l*. in one year. The ordinary pay of workmen in their position would rarely exceed 50*l*. or 60*l*. a year. The masters also are put in a very difficult position; if they allow this inequality, all the other workmen are certain to demand an increase of pay; if they try to reduce the rate of wage earned by the men who work this machinery, they are met by the obstinate resistance of the men so employed.

Quarrels between masters and men arise also from other causes; and sometimes the men can allege serious grievances in justification of their complaints.

The iniquitous institution called the Truck Shop was a grievance of very old standing. This was a shop established by the proprietor on the premises, where he sold to his workmen provisions, meat, groceries, liquor, &c., on credit, and at exorbitant prices, frequently using threats to drive them to increased consumption, and keeping back out of their wages to the amount that he had thus extorted. The more intelligent among the workmen stoutly resisted this exaction, and often even went on strike to oblige the masters to abandon it. Public opinion was aroused; and at last Parliament, struck by the monstrous abuses caused by the system, forbade it absolutely. Even now, however, the workmen are sometimes obliged to resist attempts to re-establish the Truck Shop under a disguised form.

One condition of piecework is, that if a product is defective, the wages of those out of whose hands it comes are kept back. This rule, although necessary in principle, has sometimes led to abuses, of which the workmen complain bitterly. The process of galvanizing a sheet of iron causes certain defects to appear in the quality of the metal, which it was impossible to discover before: if the sheet, under these circumstances, is condemned, and the wages of the rollers kept back, these men have to suffer loss solely from the fault of the puddler who prepared the metal. The workmen accuse the masters of sometimes withholding the whole of their wages, even when there is not a total loss, but only a reduced profit on a defective product.

There are also circumstances for which the sliding-scale does not provide. A certain description of pig-iron, very difficult to puddle, may, in the form of bars, fetch less than another easier to work, or where the yield of metal has been larger. The workmen who have prepared the first, think that they have a right to a higher rate of pay than that which is allowed an ordinary puddler.

The puddlers are sometimes fined, when the products turned out by them have been pronounced to be defective. The law forbids this practice; but a number of workmen asserted before the Commission that it still exists, and that the managers keep back so large a part of their pay to meet these arbitrary fines, that sometimes the men get next to nothing: if a man protested, they say, he would be instantly discharged. Such cases must be rare, but it does not take much to arouse the workmen's ever-watchful mistrust. In this, as in all other trades, the mere fact of the existence of Unions is frequently the origin of many disputes. Some masters affect to ignore them, and refuse to receive their representatives. Others go still farther, and rigorously exclude all Union men from their works. Some even have been reproached with having, without the excuse of an example first set by the men, drawn up black lists, the fatal effects of which we have already pointed out. From all these causes numerous strikes have occurred. There are cases in which workmen have persecuted their fellows for not joining in strikes, and in which masters have persecuted the men who took a leading part in managing them; but the evidence collected by the Commission, and the discussions held in public before it, both prove that the grievances alleged on both sides were exaggerated. None of the protective rules, which some of the Unions in other trades attempted to enforce, are met with in the iron industry.

No fixed period of service is imposed on the apprentices, nor is their number limited. Moreover, the members of Unions do not refuse to work in the same establishments with non-Unionists; in fact they both almost always make common cause together. Lastly, the masters themselves admit that in several instances the Unions have exercised a beneficial influence over the workmen; they refuse to allow rattening, and they have abolished the fraudulent custom of secreting pieces of iron to throw into the furnace in order to increase the yield.

The Unions now existing among the iron-workers are all of recent origin. A society was founded in 1845, but being unable to resist the masters, who obliged their workmen to abandon it, it was dissolved in 1847. In 1857, the year when the first advance of sixpence was made to the rate of pay of the puddlers, no Union existed. The National Association of Iron-workers, composed principally of puddlers, was founded in 1862, and its head-quarters were established in the north, at Gateshead. The society called the Associated Iron-workers of Great Britain, which chose the town of Brierley Hill as its head-quarters, was established the following year, in the midst of a strike, whose success it caused. All the puddlers in England entered the ranks of one or other of these societies, those of each district generally dividing themselves between the two. The Gateshead society comprised 450 members in North Staffordshire; that of Brierley Hill 350. In June, 1864, the two Unions made an effort to amalgamate; in this they did not succeed, but they engaged always to stand by one another. The prosperity of the trade just at this time made them very strong; puddlers were receiving at the rate of ten shillings and sixpence per ton, a higher rate than they have ever obtained either before or since. Most of the rollers were also members of some Union: their most important Union was established also at Gateshead, and consisted of between five and six thousand members; and, seeing that whenever the Union struck, ten men were thrown out of work for each individual roller on strike, it must have possessed immense influence over the whole trade. The members of Unions in all the branches might be reckoned at about three-fourths of the total number of iron-workers.

While the men were thus fortifying themselves by means of their associations, the masters had also adopted similiar measures by way of defence. For fifty years a Masters' Association has existed in Staffordshire, designed, among other objects, to regulate wages and secure their uniformity. In the north of England the proprietors of blast furnaces and those of forges have each their society. That belonging to the forge proprietors, called the North of England Iron Manufacturers' Association, is a genuine Trade Union, with all the features which distinguish the workmen's societies. Each proprietor insures all or a certain number of his puddling furnaces against the effects of a strike by undertaking in writing, on the requisition of the secretary, to pay a sum determined by the number of furnaces so insured, and the amount of yield assigned to each. If his workmen leave him, the Association pays him, according to the sum for which he is insured, 4*l*. or 3*l*. a week for each furnace: this allowance is raised out of the funds subscribed by the other members. The funds at the disposal of this Society amounted, on December 1, 1866, to nearly 48,000*l*.

The masters' Unions in Staffordshire, though less

strongly organized, were animated by the same spirit. No one of the members was allowed to pay his workmen in excess of the tariff which the Association had fixed by the sliding-scale ; they drew together in closer alliance, and eventually, by turning against the workmen their own weapons, succeeded in subduing all resistance to their will. They soon began to take the offensive; in the Leeds district a lock-out was proclaimed in the spring of 1864, for the purpose of compelling the workmen to abandon the Unions recently introduced among them. The Gateshead and Brierley Hill Associations united to resist this; but they spent 17,000*l*. and kept up the struggle for six months to no purpose. They were conquered by an importation of Belgian workmen, who supplied the place of the men on strike.

The great prosperity, which enabled the Unions to obtain such high pay for the men in 1863, had but a short run. About the middle of the following year the Staffordshire proprietors found themselves compelled to lower the price of their iron. But, relying on a speedy revival of business, they judged it more prudent not to reduce their payments in proportion : the workmen, therefore, supposed that the rate of wages would not be altered unless the price of iron sunk still lower, so that when the reduction, which had been so unwisely put off, became at last necessary, it was looked upon as a cruel injustice by the men, who could not have complained if it had been made a few months earlier. The masters had foreseen this resistance, and had prepared for it in December 1864, by entering into an agreement with the manufacturers throughout England that a general reduction of wages should take place simultaneously all over the country, and that they should all stand by one another in case of need. They accordingly announced that, from and after the 14th of January, 1865, one shilling should be taken off the pay of the puddlers, and that all other wages should be reduced ten per cent. There was a great stir among all the operatives, the puddlers especially. Delegates from the two puddlers' Unions attended a conference held at Sheffield, at which, without agreeing to any common plan of operations, it was decided that, a fight being out of the question, the men should do their best to obtain favourable terms, and should, at any sacrifice, avoid an useless strike. A special meeting of delegates from all the branches of the Brierley Hill Society confirmed this decision, and at the same time authorized the North Staffordshire puddlers only, on the ground that living was dearer in their district than in any other, to propose to the masters that the reduction should be limited to sixpence. They thought that this proposal would be accepted; and, contrary to the wishes of the workmen in the rest of the county, the society promised to support the puddlers if they met with a refusal. Their offer was refused, and they went on strike on the day appointed for the reduction. All their fellow-workmen in the iron works, who belonged to the Gateshead Union, did the same; but this society, in order to mark its disapproval of disobedience to orders, soon ceased to allow them any assistance. Depending on what casual aid they could obtain, they soon came to an open rupture with their association, and allied themselves to the puddlers belonging to the Brierley Hill Society, who helped them as well as they were able out of the small resources at their disposal. In spite of warnings received from the leading men of both associations, in spite of the offer of Lord Lichfield, Lord-Lieutenant of the county, to act as arbitrator, these 800 puddlers persisted obstinately in their course.

The Brierley Hill Union continuing to assist them, the South Staffordshire masters resolved to put an end to this, and to join their brethren of the north of the county in compelling the resisting workmen to accept the reduction: they closed all their establishments on the 6th of March, and announced that they would not resume work until the men had submitted to the terms proposed. The midland and northern proprietors were requested to come to the support of the factories affected by the strike, which the Gateshead Union was accused of secretly encouraging. These met at York, and proclaimed a lock-out on the 17th of March. The result was that all the puddling furnaces in England were extinguished at once; for a whole fortnight the great iron trade ceased to exist; it has never completely recovered from the effects of the shock. This state of affairs, however, could not last long. The Gateshead Society, which was always opposed to and had never joined in the strike, had no objection to give the promise exacted by the North of England Iron Manufacturers' Association; whereupon the latter immediately threw open their establishments. The Brierley Hill Association, seeing that resistance was useless, had ceased, ever since the lock-out, to give any assistance to the North Staffordshire puddlers, who began the strife, and had, though in vain, recommended them to give in. Upon this, the proprietors in the south of the county, who were bound by their engagements with their brethren in the north, asked their northern brethren's permission also to resume work, without waiting for the strike to come to an end. The fact is, public opinion was beginning to find fault with the lock-out, which threatened not only to ruin the iron trade, but caused extreme distress among a numerous and industrious population, which had never been mixed up in the quarrel and entirely disapproved of it. The iron-masters too, had no wish to prolong this state of affairs; they met accordingly at Wolverhampton, and, on the 5th of April, declared the lock-out at an end.

For all this, the North Staffordshire workmen persisted: they appealed to the public for subscriptions, and were encouraged by promises from Mr. Potter, and the London Society of which he is the secretary. But no money came in; until at last, reduced to utter misery, they were obliged to yield. The loss in wages from this strike may be reckoned at 120,000*l*.; by the lockout the iron-masters prevented the men from earning 150,000*l*. in South Staffordshire, and 50,000*l*. in the North of England: so that the workmen lost 320,000*l*. in wages alone by this disastrous struggle, without counting what it cost the funds of their associations. The losings of the masters were as great, and both parties still feel its effects.

The importance of this strike throws all subsequent strikes into the shade. It will be enough, therefore, merely to give a rapid sketch of a few of them.

The first we have occasion to mention, broke out among the rollers of North Staffordshire on account of the terms on which they were taken on again after the return of the puddlers to work: they succeeded in obtaining the wages which they asked for.*

In May, 1866, the puddlers at the Mersey Iron-works

---

* They had taken no part in the puddlers' strike, and belonged to a separate Union of their own, which is a purely trade society, and has one peculiar feature: it has two rates of subscription, and the members get more or less assistance when they are not at work, according to the rate at which they have subscribed.—*Author's Note*.

(Liverpool), were thrown out of work in consequence of a strike among the labourers. The proprietors took advantage of this, and, on work being resumed, exacted from them a promise that they would leave the Union. This they refused to do, upon which the manager of the works, Mr. Clay, undertook to do without them; he set to work himself, and had men, picked up anywhere, taught to act as puddlers, and was so successful that he managed to set eighteen furnaces going, and obliged the puddlers to capitulate. The leaders were discharged; the rest were compelled to have their names struck off the list of their association; and thus, being deprived of all means of defence, they had thenceforth no power of opposing the employers. One day several of these men were absent from the works without having given any previous notice, and on their being acquitted by the court, before which the manager of the works prosecuted them, he immediately closed the establishment, and would take back only those workmen who engaged to give a week's notice before leaving. But the most serious strike in the North of England was one which, beginning on the 14th of July, 1866, lasted five months, and deprived, during its continuance, twelve thousand men of work. All these sufferings were to no purpose; the trade sunk lower and lower, and they had to accept the reduction of wages which they had previously rejected.

There are Unions also in the iron-founders' trade

(producers of pig-iron), which is intimately connected with the wrought-iron trade, and supplies the latter with the raw material; but the former has never been disturbed by strikes on so grand a scale as those we have been describing. The honour of this happy result may be ascribed partly to the chief Union in this trade, called the "Friendly Society of Ironfounders," which is as prudent as it is ancient and powerful. Having been founded fifty-nine years ago, it was, of course, until 1824, a secret society. Its members used to choose a dark night for their meetings, which were held on one of the peaty wastes called moors, which spread over the high ground in the midland counties. There they collected the subscriptions towards the common fund; there they concerted measures for the strike which was to break out without any appearance of a common understanding among the men; and there relief was distributed after they had thrown up work. Before the day broke upon these innocent conspiracies, before the early call of the grouse, sole inhabitant of these vast deserts, attracted the sportsman to its haunts, the archives of the society were carefully buried, and every one made his way to the neighbouring town.

This society is spread now all over England, Ireland, and Wales; it numbers more than eleven thousand members, and in 1865 its receipts rose to 36,297*l*. But experience has brought prudence; it does not despise in its strength the conditions necessary to ensure success. The secretary himself has declared that a strike ought never to be allowed to last more than six weeks, and that if at the end of that time the workmen have not carried their point, it is best for them to give in.

It has been already observed that the argument entered into between the two great parties before the Commission related to the highest interests of the great industry by which both earn their living; and the question of what is a fair rate of wages was the subject discussed by both sides with the greatest eagerness. Each reproached the other with wishing to appropriate exclusively to itself — by unduly raising or unduly lowering wages—all the profits, which are the fruit of their joint efforts. The masters accused the Unions of causing the decay of their trade by exacting an excessive and untimely increase of pay. The workmen, on the other hand, reproached the masters with using these complaints only as a veil to conceal the large profits, which they still believe the latter are making. The conclusion we draw from these arguments is that both these opposite imputations are equally unfounded. The decay of the iron trade is an undoubted fact, but the Unions cannot be held answerable for it.

The real causes of this decay are, first, the excess of capital invested in the trade, followed by over-production : secondly, and unfortunately simultaneously, a sudden and extraordinary diminution of consumption. It is remarkable that, although there was a large increase in the exports of English iron during the years 1864 and 1865 (the excess of 1865 over preceding years amounted to nearly 1,500,000*l.*), the home consumption during this period diminished in a much larger proportion. This diminution cannot be attributed to the high wages paid, because, if so, the exports would have been the first to be affected;* it is generally attributed to the stoppage of railway works and of iron shipbuilding, and to the great financial crisis, which has shaken confidence and caused the suspension of all enterprises in which long credit is required.

The rate of wages is affected by the Unions only to the extent stated in the preceding chapter: they can, in some degree, regulate its fluctuations; they can retard a fall, and slightly accelerate a rise ; but it is as impossible for them to change the law of these fluctuations as it is for a man on a field of battle to stop with his

---

* As it has been asserted that the importation of Belgian iron is a proof of the injury caused by high wages to the trade in England, it is worth while to expose the fallacy of this statement. The imports of Belgian iron have been to the value of 1,946*l.* in 1863; 75,848*l.* in 1864; 99,950*l.* in 1865; while in 1865 alone the value of English iron exported amounted to the enormous sum of 17,000,950*l.*, that is to say, about 18,000,000*l.* exported, to 100,000*l.* imported. These figures give one an idea of the importance of this branch of trade.—*Author's Note.*

hand one of those spent balls which go turning over and over, smashing everything they touch. Were it otherwise, how comes it that the wages of the ten thousand workmen in Wales, who have no Union to fall back upon, are very little lower than those of their brethren in England? Every one must admit the importance of the influence which the fluctuations in the rate of wages exert on prices, and on the prosperity of an industry such as the iron trade; but these fluctuations are small. Almost all employers acknowledge that there is a minimum below which wages must not be allowed to drop. Lord Dudley's agent, Mr. Smith, who holds a leading position in the trade, has declared that he will never consent to reduce them below seven-and-sixpence, and that he should prefer the present rate of eight shillings and sixpence to be the minimum. "I do not wish," he very justly remarks, "ever to see a puddler working at a less rate of wages than he is at the present time, even though, unfortunately, the price of iron should have to be reduced; because the moment you bring a class of men like the puddlers, who are very hard-worked, below a certain rate of wages, that moment you rid the community of the best men."*

* Iron-masters often go on working at a loss; they find that as long they are not losing more than ten shillings per ton, this is better than stopping their works. They then, as they are doing now, reduce their production to a minimum by working only three days a-week.—*Author's Note.*

The employers, moreover, perceive that interests of a higher order forbid, above all things, the excessive depreciation of the value of labour. In short, everything proves that the degree to which the men will be steady, well-conducted, and reasonable, is in exact proportion to the remuneration which they receive. "I believe," remarks an iron-moulder, "that nothing but England's well-paid artisans maintained our position as a nation during the great struggle and crisis of revolutions on the Continent. And you will recollect further, that at the time when the Chartist agitation was going on in this country, their cry was, Only pull down the artisan class of this country to the level of the labourer, and the charter would have to be granted."

On the other hand, it may be asserted that, taking into account even the highest rate of wages prevailing in times of the greatest prosperity, their general average is decidedly low. The proprietors are able to set aside a certain portion out of their share in the profits as an insurance fund against bad years; the workman cannot spare out of his share, represented by his wages, anything like a relative portion for insurance. The examples of very high wages which have been quoted are exceptions, and arose out of peculiar circumstances. We have already mentioned one of these instances, that of the rollers who earned 400*l.* and 450*l.* pounds a-year; and it was proved that this sudden rise was owing to improvements in machinery. When, however, a trade makes a sudden advance like this, the public do not always immediately profit by the diminished cost of production; the benefit of this goes either to the masters, if they are not obliged to pay higher wages, or to the workmen, if, as in the case of the rollers, they continue with less labour to obtain the same share in the value of the product. But the balance is soon restored; and, in the end, the benefits of every invention are always shared between the public and the producers. The masters and the workmen make a fresh division of the share in these benefits accruing to each, regulated by the prices offered and the demand for the article; and the operatives have never been liable to the charge of monopolizing the whole of such share.

Other cases, similar to that of the rollers, prove only that, even in this laborious trade, intelligence is a much more valuable quality in a workman than mere muscular strength. The chief hammermen in the Mersey Ironworks are allowed from 3*l*. to 3*l*. 10*s*. a week for the work of the apprentices under them, out of which they pay the apprentices only 1*l*. a week. The hammermen themselves, who are paid by the day, earn by their own work from 11*l*. 10*s*. to 12*l*. 10*s*. a week; so that, with this and with what they can make out of the apprentice allowance, their annual income amounts to 700*l*. or 900*l*. But, at the same time, a great responsibility is laid upon them. A single misdirected blow of the steam-hammer may entirely spoil the work in hand, which may be an enormous screw-shaft for a great ship of war, worth 2,500*l.* or 3,500*l.* A workman, therefore, on whose skill and correct eye the reputation of the whole factory often depends, has a right to put a high value on his services. But these, as we have said, are rare exceptions. The average of wages earned by a good puddler rarely exceeds 60*l.*, and scarcely ever reaches 75*l.* a year, even under the most favourable circumstances. With a maximum and a minimum so little apart there is no room for any considerable fluctuations in the value of labour, which, consequently, is but slightly affected by them.

The speakers, in the course of this discussion, constantly appealed, in support of their arguments, to the rules and customs by which trade is governed among other manufacturing nations; and both masters and workmen being equally anxious that this larger field of inquiry should be included within the scope of the Commission, the Commissioners acquiesced, and by so doing were preserved from taking a too exclusively English view of the wages question.

Their attention was especially drawn to the position of the Unions in the United States, the only country which has as yet adopted them. Much valuable information is contained in the evidence of Mr. Hewitt, the American iron-master, whom we have quoted before, and who is well known for his kind treatment of his workmen. The American Unions are purely trade societies, and, therefore, do not raise any relief fund.* They are very rarely called upon to resist a reduction of wages, and strikes are almost unknown. The only strike upon record in the iron trade is that of the puddlers in Pennsylvania, among whom, Mr. Hewitt says, there were scarcely any Americans; they were almost all Irishmen, brought up in the tradition that a strike is the natural weapon of the workman against his master. During the civil war the Federal Government was in such haste to get its orders executed that workmen could obtain almost anything they liked to ask. But the high rate of wages prevailing in America is not to be ascribed to any mere temporary state of affairs like this. The low price of land acts as an infallible remedy to the depreciation of labour. In a country where any man can buy land from the State at an almost nominal price, to be paid in small yearly instalments, the iron worker leaves the forge the moment he has discovered that his pay is less than what he would gain by cultivat-

---

* The English law, cancelling all contracts and agreements "in restraint of trade," remains in force in America, but it would appear never to have been applied to the Unions, which there enjoy almost all the rights and privileges for which they are now striving in England. In the state of New York they are recognized as corporations, and may hold property by corporate title.—*Author's Note.*

ing his own land. To Americans, without any home or trade ties, the prospect of becoming proprietors in the far west is so dazzling that they can be induced to go on working for wages only by the offer of very preponderating advantages. The result is, that in the iron trade labour is three and four times dearer than in England, although the cost of living is by no means greater in the same proportion. This high price of labour is the cause not only of the necessity for protecting the native manufacture in spite of its magnificent natural advantages, but also of the peculiar part assigned to America in the economy of the civilized world. As the facilities of Transatlantic intercourse increase, the prejudices and traditions which bind down the European to spots in which he finds it hard to earn a living will vanish, and the ties of country, noble as they are, will give way before the sense of unfair treatment and the increasing attractions of the great republic. It will then become necessary, in order to keep men at home, to ensure them the same advantages as they would find in emigration, and thus the balance of wages will be restored naturally on both sides of the Atlantic. The reason why America is for the present obliged to resort to protection is because it is easier to import iron from England than men; consequently, as the men stay at home and work on lower wages than their American brethren, the iron which they turn out can be sold cheaper than the products of the Pennsylvanian forges. But emigration is daily tending more and more to make the wages of labour the same in all countries;* that is to say, of intelligent, experienced and skilled labour, the value of which increases in proportion as the self-acting work of machinery is substituted by the progress of civilization for rude manual labour, requiring only a certain amount of muscular strength. In these respects England is placed, commercially as well as geographically, between America on the one side, and France, Belgium and Germany on the other,—a singularly favourable position to occupy at the present time: she is protected against the formidable competition of America by the high wages prevailing there; and against that of the continent, where the value of labour and the cost of living is less, and the wants of the workman are fewer than in England, by the difficulties, which the situation of the various beds opposes to the successful working of the mineral wealth contained in them.†

* Accordingly a great many English Unions raise a special fund for the encouragement of emigration.—*Author's Note.*

† Belgium, in which minerals abound more than in any other continental state, can compete with only one class of English iron, that produced in Staffordshire. The difficulties of transport, against which mining industry has to struggle in France, are well known; it is satisfactory, therefore, that Mr. Hewitt should have done full justice to it by declaring before the Commission, that the Creuzot establishment was prevented only by these difficulties from yielding products quite equal to the best English specimens, and at lower prices.—*Author's Note.*

This tendency to a gradual rise in wages is simultaneously apparent all over the world. In France the introduction of highly-paid English puddlers has enabled the French puddlers, in the opinion even of foreigners like Mr. Hewitt, to equal the English in skill, and so to command wages as high as those paid at Liverpool and in Staffordshire. On the other hand, in certain districts in England, where the pay of purely manual labour is very low, it may fairly be expected that the masters will consent to waive the advantage this gives them over the market, and will adopt a fairer scale of remuneration. This advantage was, in fact, obtained only by putting women to the rudest and hardest work; at the great works at Merthyr Tydvil, for instance, women are employed to stack large bars of iron, after they have been hammered; for this labour, which no strong healthy man would undertake for less than two shillings and threepence, they are paid a shilling a day. This mischievous practice is condemned by public opinion as unjust both to the women, who receive so poor a return for their hard toil, and to the men, whose wages suffer from their having to compete with women.

CHAPTER VI.

THE COAL TRADE.

THERE is a natural connection between the coal and the iron trade, and the population employed in it is quite as interesting a race of men as the iron-workers.

It has been truly remarked that a lump of coal is a bottled sunbeam : a sunbeam is the varying, indestructible, prolific agent, which we call light, heat, chemical action, electricity and motion. But few are aware what toils and dangers have to be undergone by a whole population, in order to get at these precious remains of a former vegetation buried under the surface of the earth, which, as fuel and gas-light, give back to us the active elements of life which were spread over the globe long before the creation of man.

Shafts of immense depth form the only communication between the outer world and the labyrinth of low, narrow galleries, through which the hard-working race employed in this branch of labour is incessantly moving. In spite of all improvements in ventilation, the atmosphere in these subterranean hives is stifling, and the terrible fire-damp, leaking through invisible cracks, is ever ready to visit a single moment's negligence with fatal consequences. Against this destructive agent the utmost precautions are of no avail; it is always liable to break forth from any fresh-made opening, in which it had been shut up for hundreds of centuries. The men are sometimes crushed by the soil falling in, when, after working at a layer of coal as hard as stone, they come suddenly upon a seam as friable as touchwood. The following figures will give an idea both of the importance and the dangers of the miners' calling:—Out of 174,000,000 tons of coal brought into the market in 1867, 101,000,000 came from England. This quantity was the produce of 3,195 mines, in which 282,000 men were employed. During this year, 1867, there were 1,190 deaths caused by accident (in 1866 there had been 1,484), 286 of which were owing to fire-damp. In one year, therefore, in this dangerous work, one man was killed out of every 280, and a life was sacrificed for every 88,000 tons of coal raised.

In reading their evidence before the Royal Commission it is impossible not to feel admiration and sympathy for the determined hardy men bred by this life of toil, privation, and risk. We have hitherto refrained, as a rule, from mentioning individuals, confining our attention to the more general features of the subject in hand;

but it would be conveying a very imperfect idea of the influence of Trades' Unions and of the future before them, if we omitted to notice some of their leading men, who are an honour to the cause which they represent.

One of these, Mr. McDonald, told the story of his life with striking simplicity. He was born in Scotland forty years ago, and at the age of eight began to work in an iron mine. He was obliged, summer and winter, to get up at two o'clock in the morning, and never returned home till seven o'clock the following evening. For sixteen or seventeen hours he was employed in pushing along trucks in galleries often only eighteen inches high, and so badly ventilated, and charged to such a degree with carbonic acid gas, that three or four lamps placed close together did not afford sufficient light for loading the ore. Not one of the twenty other children, who were McDonald's companions in the mine, lived to grow up. In the second mine in which he worked there were thirty boys, and a good many girls. All these, with the exception of himself and his brother, died quite young, broken down by hard work, and extinguished, like one of their own wretched lamps, by the poisonous atmosphere. Nevertheless, so great was his desire to obtain higher pay and an improved position, that in spite of these terrible trials, and almost before he had fairly attained manhood, McDonald devoted himself to miner's work in its most laborious form. He undertook by contract to construct the galleries by tunnelling through the rock (called running a level) in places where he had to work up to his knees in water, and with the moisture from the walls incessantly dripping upon him. He says himself " in the morning when I entered, the first thing that I always did was to roll myself all over right in the water, and wet every part of the body, for the express purpose that the water falling from the roof should not create the very unpleasant sensation which water does to one who has gone recently from his bed into the mine that is wet." The toilsome life he led did not prevent him from attending the night school which had been recently set up for the benefit of the workmen. Having saved a little money by the time he was one-and-twenty, he resolved on dividing his time; during the summer he continued to work with his hands, in the winter he went to the University of Glasgow, where he studied Greek, Latin, Rhetoric and Mathematics: the six months spent thus cost him about 60*l*. At last, after having been foreman of a mine, he dropped the pickaxe and mattock to become secretary of an Union. The confidence placed in him by all his fellow-workmen has since called him to the position he now occupies,—that of President of the National Association of Miners, a vast society which embraces all the pitmens' Unions in the three kingdoms.

Other workmen, from the same beginnings, and equally energetic and persevering, have followed another line, and ended by becoming masters. Twenty-seven or twenty-eight years ago, among the wretched children of eight or ten at work in mines, was one called George Elliot. Subsequently, he took part as a miner in the great strikes, by means of which the workmen obtained a large reduction in the hours of labour; he still speaks of this as one of the most precious victories obtained by justice and humanity. From the time he was twenty, owing to his keen intelligence, he began to rise above the condition of a simple miner. After passing through all the subordinate steps in a miner's calling, he became foreman, then manager, and is now one of the chief proprietors in England, and owns mines situated in several districts. In the mines of which he is owner, together with those which he manages as agent, he employs ten thousand men, and raises annually two million tons of coal: that is to say, an eightieth part of all that is produced throughout the world. Never forgetful of his origin, he has always been on the best terms with his workmen. He ends his evidence in the following words :—" I do not think there is a finer body of men in the world than the pitmen in the country, and I think if you can inspire them with the feeling that you are fair, and intend nothing but what is just towards them, you can manage them."

In the coal-pits all payments are made by piecework. The galleries are so low that the workmen are obliged to strike the vein of coal with their picks lying down on their backs; the lumps so detached are then packed upon trucks, which are simply boxes on wheels. The trucks are pushed along a tramway to the end of the gallery, and thence hoisted to the surface by a steam-engine, where their load is weighed, and each workman is credited with the amount he has contributed to the product, and is paid so much for every ton of coal raised. In some pits — at Staveley for instance — a certain number of men take a gallery under contract, and work it as partners, taking their chance of loss or gain according to the quality of the seam. In other pits the comparative facility of the work depends on this quality; the miners therefore in some galleries are paid more per ton than those in others of the same pit. In Durham and Northumberland the pitmen are engaged by the year at a fixed salary, the owner guaranteeing them a minimum of from thirty to thirty-three shillings per fortnight, whether they are at work or not. This old-fashioned system, though it has at different times been found fault with both by employers and by the Unions, is, on the whole, advantageous to both parties: to the masters, because it ensures them against a sudden rise in wages, which is fatal in cases where they have undertaken contracts in which the payment is long deferred; to the workmen, because it secures them from want of employment and the misery caused by it.

Following the development of the Union system in this branch of industry, we shall point out the various objects at which it aimed, and the improvements which it has accomplished in the miners' existence.

Unions were established first in Scotland. Enough has been said to show the miserable condition at that time of the workers in the pits, but even this was a great improvement on what that condition had been previously. Down to 1779 it was literally a state of serfdom. The miners were compelled by law to remain in the pits as long as the owner chose to keep them at work there, and were actually sold as part of the capital invested in the works. If they accepted an engagement elsewhere their master could always have them fetched back and flogged as thieves for having attempted to rob him of their labour. This law was modified in 1779, but was not repealed till after the Acts passed in 1797 and 1799. The abuses, however, of which the workmen were victims, did not disappear all at once: the combination laws were in full force: truck-shops were everywhere established, and in order to oblige their workmen to resort to them and purchase on credit, the masters paid the men only at long intervals.*

* Since the abolition of truck-shops, this deferred payment has given rise to another sort of abuse, of which the workmen still complain bitterly. When a labourer is earning 3*l.* per fortnight, he may, though he is not paid until the last day of the fortnight, consider himself the lawful owner of 30*s.* at the end of the first week. But, if he

The underground galleries were crowded with women and children, the latter in a state of utter ignorance: the men were kept at work sometimes more than sixteen hours out of the twenty-four, and nothing was done towards either the healthiness or the safety of the mines. Accordingly the societies, established before the relieving Acts above mentioned, grew in strength, and ended by defying the law. The Lanarkshire Miners' Union had been openly tolerated since 1817; and this example had its influence on the act of justice which was carried out by the abolition of the penalties against combination in 1824. As soon as this was accomplished, the societies set themselves to attack the customs, which, as old-fashioned relics of serfdom, they looked upon as fatal to the position of the workman, and with this view they endeavoured to interest public opinion in their favour. It would be an exaggeration to attribute all that has been done in England towards rooting out these abuses and improving the miners' condition to the sole influence of these societies, but it is certain that by their persevering defence of their legitimate interests both before the public and before parliamentary com-

---

then wants to be paid, say, 1*l.* out of this sum of 30*s.*, which clearly belongs to him, it is the practice, in some works, to make him sign a receipt for a guinea. The extra shilling represents interest on the advance of the 1*l.*, which he, nevertheless, had already lawfully earned. This amounts to making him pay five per cent. per week, which is equivalent to 260*l.* per cent. per annum.—*Author's Note.*

missions they have hastened the progress of legislation, and are now at last beginning to feel the beneficial effect of their efforts. They have had to conquer the force of tradition, the aversion—generally well founded—of the English people to any legal interference, and lastly, the opposition of a great number of masters. While they were accomplishing this work, sometimes by means of petitioning Parliament, sometimes by striking, they were also engaged in other, often long and furious, contests, either to obtain an increase, or to resist a reduction of wages, or in defence of their very existence. But they cannot be accused of having either introduced or spread a habit of striking among the workmen, for the most violent and obstinate strikes have broken out in places where Unions have never existed; on the other hand, they have had a large share in promoting every one of the social improvements which it is the pride of our time to have secured to the class of miners in England.

Their first efforts were crowned with success. They obtained a parliamentary inquiry into the truck-shop system, the result of which was that Lord Ashley (now Lord Shaftesbury) introduced a measure in the House of Commons, which was carried in 1831, absolutely forbidding this usurious practice.

In this same year, 1831, the English miners made use, for the first time, of the right of combining: but they established only a temporary league, and their

Unions seem not to have assumed the same shape as those in Scotland. They wanted to obtain a reduction of the number of hours to a day's work.* A workman named Tommy Hepburn, put himself at their head; he was gifted with rare intelligence, and possessed of all the qualities which make a man a leader among his fellows. Thirty thousand workmen struck in Durham and Northumberland; after much suffering they ended by carrying their point; and the day's work was reduced to twelve hours. This reduction was as beneficial to the masters, who had opposed it, as to the workmen: the latter worked with increased energy, and the yield of the mines became larger. The workmen were not satisfied with this success, but went on to demand a considerable rise in their wages. Hepburn tried in vain to dissuade them from this, they insisted, and went on strike; but the anticipations of their chief were soon realized, and in a short time they were obliged to give in.

Not long after these events the Unions, being now fully organized in the north of England, applied, in

* Although payment is by piece-work, still the discipline indispensable in a mine makes it necessary that the number of working hours should be fixed. In mines where labour is not continuous, the men employed in the carriage of ore along the galleries, and in attending to the hoisting engines, must work a certain time, and if a miner leaves off sooner, it is a clear loss to the owner. In those where labour is carried on uninterruptedly, it is necessary that every workman should know the hour at which he has to go and take the place of the man whom he relieves.—*Author's Note.*

concert with those of Scotland, for legislative interference to protect the workmen from the bad ventilation of mines and to stop the employment of women and children.

The subject was referred in 1834 to a Parliamentary Committee, which issued some recommendations merely, and these do not seem to have been much attended to. At last, in 1842, both Houses having become alive to the fatal consequences of these growing abuses, passed an act absolutely forbidding underground labour to women, and children under the age of twelve.*

After this, with the exception of one unimportant strike in Derbyshire, work went on in the coal pits without any disturbance until 1844. In this year the miners in the counties of Durham and Northumberland refused to go up and down the shafts by means of the newly introduced iron-wire cables, believing the old-fashioned ropes of hemp to be safer. They soon gave up striving for this, but remained upon strike in order to enforce the continuance of the system of engagements by the year, in the accomplishment of which, however, after standing out four months, they also failed.

This defeat put an end to the Unions in these districts for a time, but after the lapse of five years they sprang up again, and renewed the fight in 1849. Taught

* Up to the passing of this Act, the women employed in the Scotch coal-pits were made to ascend from the bottom to the surface by means of perpendicular slippery ladders, with a load of 200 pounds of coal on their backs.—*Author's Note.*

by experience, the workmen attacked only one mine at a time; and in order to reduce it to submission, the men employed in it, instead of striking, reduced their labour, and consequently the yield, so as to earn only first three shillings, then two, and at last only one shilling a day. Through this system, called restriction, the yield of the mine fell to next to nothing, while all the general working expenses remained undiminished; the other miners contributed to the support of the men working in the mine under restriction, whose presence, though their work was merely nominal, was an obstacle to fresh hands being called in. This mode of proceeding was adopted at the Marley Hill coal pit. The directors, not choosing to put up with this treatment, discharged all their workmen, turned them out of the houses they had let to them, and ended by having Scotch miners fetched to supply their place. These measures succeeded, and after a fruitless resistance, the men originally employed in the pit were compelled to ask leave to resume work in it, and to abandon their claim for increased pay.

From this time strikes increased in frequency, even in places where the Unions possessed small influence. In the Leeds district, in which out of 7,000 workmen only 2,000 were members of Unions, a dispute, ending in a strike for increased pay, broke out in 1853, between Messrs. Pope and Pearson and their workmen. On this occasion, although Messrs. Pope and Pearson received the support of the neighbouring employers, the men carried their point, after standing out five months.

During the year 1855 twelve strikes occurred in Durham. There were a great many also in Scotland: one of these, in Lanarkshire, began in 1856, and lasted thirteen months; it ended in the success of the masters. In the Leeds district, again, hostilities were renewed in 1858. All the workmen combined to establish an Union, which took the name of the South Yorkshire Miners' Association, for the assistance of their brethren belonging to Mr. Briggs' extensive coal works. He, in his turn, was backed by the members of his class, and the allied masters proclaimed a lock-out. After two months, during which the men lost about 40,000*l.*, both parties came to a compromise, as they ought to have done in the beginning. The masters wanted to reduce wages fifteen per cent.; the men wanted to keep them as they were: at last both parties agreed to a reduction of seven-and-a-half per cent.

There was a rise shortly, but this did not prevent a contest from breaking out on a fresh subject. The efforts of the workmen were this time directed against "confiscation"—a practice of which they have never ceased to complain, and which, more than any other perhaps, causes irritation against the owners of mines. Every time a tub of coal on coming to bank was found, on weighing, to be under a certain weight, or to contain a certain proportion of earth or stone mixed with the coal, it was declared forfeited, the contents were emptied into the depôt, but it was not carried to the credit of the pitman who sent it up, and he received no payment for his labour. The workmen declare that a tub has been forfeited when only a single lump of coal has happened to fall out on its way to the pit's mouth, and that sometimes, in consequence of errors, accidental or otherwise, tubs of the required weight have been confiscated, and this to such an extent as in some collieries to amount to one-twelfth part of all the coal raised. To get rid of this system, which in certain cases may be necessary, but is clearly liable to great abuse, the workmen struck. All the masters in the district combined in its defence, and gave notice of another lock-out. Eighteen collieries were simultaneously closed, thereby depriving of their work more than 10,000 men. But notwithstanding this harsh measure, the miners succeeded in the end in obtaining the redress of all their chief grievances.

All this while the Union system was acquiring strength and development among the pitmen; it was about this time, too, that it became established in the iron trade. In 1862, a large number of the hands employed in working the rich seams which lie between Liverpool and Manchester, and especially near the towns of Wigan and St. Helens, established the South Lancashire Miners' Association, in imitation of that founded at Leeds four years before. The following year Leeds was the scene of a meeting of delegates from almost all the miners' associations in England. On this occasion, Mr. McDonald represented the Scotch Unions, which had been already amalgamated, and a great society was formed under the name of the National Association of Miners, of which he was elected president. This society gave a great impulse to the diffusion of Unionist feeling. A long course of mutual annoyances and wrongs inflicted and suffered on both sides had produced a feeling of hostility between masters and workmen in Yorkshire, which needed only an excuse to break out in active war: the newly formed society furnished this excuse.

Agents of the Union were appointed, who went about in the districts in which it possessed no adherents, and addressed the workmen in passionate harangues, describing in the most glowing colours all the injuries, real or supposed, which they had received at the hands of the masters, and representing admission into the Union as an infallible remedy for all their wrongs. Two of these men, Messrs. Brown and Pickles, both of whom gave evidence before the Commission, especially distinguished themselves by their violence. It was a time when the smallest trifle caused a quarrel. At one time the masters would try to make the workmen riddle the coal underground,—this means separating the large from the small pieces by means of a sieve,—or would order the great lumps and the small coal, which had been broken in pieces, to be packed in separate tubs. At other times they would confiscate tubs though all but coming up to the required weight. This last grievance became so serious that a law was passed directing that one of the workmen in a mine, to be chosen by his companions, and paid jointly by them and the owners, should be appointed check-weigher. Several masters evaded it by immediately discharging the workman appointed to this duty, and then denying him access to the mine on the ground that he had ceased to belong to the establishment. One of the check-weighers, Mr. Normansell, now president of the South Yorkshire Union, when treated in this way, persevered in asserting his right. He allowed himself to be ejected eighteen days running from the weigh-house, and then appealed to justice. He carried his cause from court to court: and it ended by the case being brought before the Court of Queen's Bench, which ordered his employers to reinstate him in his office.[*]

The masters, on their side, prepared for the struggle and combined to establish among themselves a genuine

---

[*] The two last subjects of complaint on the part of the workmen which we need notice, were the discharge of most of the leaders of Unions, and the forced tribute levied on all miners for the pay of a medical man, in the selection of whom they had no voice.—*Author's Note.*

Union, of which one of their body, Mr. Briggs, was elected President. It was at his works that hostilities broke out in 1863 : the men there refused to adopt the system of riddling underground. He determined to conquer their resistance, and to break up the Unions, whom he accused of fomenting strikes. With this view he called in miners from the adjoining counties to supply the place of the men who had left. The old hands received the new comers with ill-concealed hostility, which the praiseworthy efforts of some of their leaders could not long keep in check. The expulsion in a body of the former tenants of the houses attached to the mine was the signal for a breakout. On the night of the 24th of September, the fresh workmen, who had been installed in these houses, were attacked, and a serious riot followed, which was with difficulty put down by the police. But this act of violence was the expiring effort of the most headstrong among the workmen on strike; after this they were obliged to own themselves beaten, to relinquish their demands, and to consent to work in company with non-Unionists. They resolved to take their revenge on the first opportunity; we shall presently see how Mr. Briggs prevented this and disarmed them as if by magic. Meanwhile, partly by intimidation, partly by persuasion, the Unions were gathering strength in the Durham collieries, and striving to obtain redress for the miners' grievances, the masters all the time endeavouring to stop their interference. The result naturally was that disputes sprung up at every turn, sometimes on the subject of forfeitures, sometimes about wages. The workmen resorted to the system of restriction, which the masters met by a lock-out. At the Brancepeth mine forty Unionist workmen and their families were turned out of some cottages in the neighbourhood of the pit which they rented from the owners. The fact that these houses remained uninhabited gave an appearance of gratuitous spite to the proceeding in the eyes of the miners, and the arrival of the strange workmen brought their irritation to a head. The police, though reinforced by special constables, could not prevent numerous riots from breaking out, and it ended by its becoming impossible for the new comers to stay in the place. The old hands were satisfied with having driven away their rivals, and resumed work without insisting on the demands they had made previously; they were no longer in a position to continue the struggle, for they had exhausted their funds and incurred a loss of 32,000*l.* in wages.

In the year 1864 the contest, which had been carried on with such vigour in South Yorkshire, assumed a different character. On this occasion the South Yorkshire Association stood aloof, and not only strongly urged the miners of the Oaks and Thorncliff collieries to abstain from a strike, but, on their persisting in this course, refused to support them, whereupon they seceded from the Association. The masters did not take advantage of the chance thus offered them of putting an end to the struggle; they combined afresh and closed all the collieries round about. It was not until 3,000 workmen, scarcely a third of whom were Unionists, were thrown out of work by this measure, that the Association decided upon assuming an attitude of resistance. The result was a complete success; after nineteen weeks the proprietors of the Oaks colliery were abandoned by their allies; and the following year the Association gathered the fruits of its timely resistance. The men at that time had demanded an advance of ten per cent. in the rate of wages, and several masters not only granted this but joined the men in measures for obtaining the same concession from other employers. Restriction was employed against the resisting masters, whose workmen reduced their labour to three shillings a day. For this the men employed in the Thorncliff colliery received their discharge, whereupon the friendly masters came to their assistance, and by contributing to the funds of the Union, enabled the workmen, after an expenditure of 5,000*l.*, to obtain a rise of wages, weekly payments, and the full recognition of the Union by the small number of proprietors who had up to that time refused to treat with its representatives.

In other places it was less successful. An attempt

was made to establish an Union in the five collieries in the neighbourhood of Chesterfield. Mr. Markham, manager of the Staveley works, resolved to oppose it. Seven or eight thousand workmen of the district having assembled to concert measures for the formation of an Union, Mr. Markham immediately discharged all who had been concerned in getting up the meeting, and threatened to do the same by any man who attended the meetings at which the Union delegates were spokesmen. Upon this the majority of the 3,000 workmen, whom he employed, left the works of their own accord, and in six weeks the colliery was all but empty. However, he would not allow that he was beaten, and attacked the Union with its own weapons. By opposing meetings by meetings, addresses by addresses, he succeeded in getting up an anti-Unionist party among the men; this was the more easy, especially with the less resolute among them, because, as the strike extended over the whole district, the men, who took part in it, received no assistance, and were reduced to extreme want. An opportunity for striking a decisive blow at last presented itself: the new enemies of the Union received a present of beef and beer; they got up a grand feast and invited their companions. This scene is described in a few words by one of them.*

* Mr. Henshaw (*Report* 6, Q. 13,801). He acknowledges that he and some others were picked out by agents of the Staveley Company,

"Three or four hundred men," he says, "that had been sticking to the Union, and who were going about with empty stomachs, when they saw this beef, were ready to swallow it whole if they could, and they all flocked in and had a share of it, and went to work the next morning."

He was asked,—"And you think the dinner had something to do with the breaking up of the Union?"

"It had a good effect, I think," was his answer, given with the utmost simplicity. This was true, for the Union was given up for the time, and Mr. Markham resumed the works at the mine with 1,500 men.

Different measures were employed to put down a strike which, in 1867, broke out in the southern part of the county. The Unionist agents had, as usual, been going about disseminating their doctrines. This brought about a combination of the masters, who discharged all the workmen belonging to the Society. This step caused great indignation. The mines were emptied, and the few workmen who ventured to stay were assailed by their companions, who called them "blood-suckers," and, armed with sticks, collected round them in threatening bands. It was impossible to come to terms when the very existence of the Unions depended upon the

and sent before the Commission as types of the anti-Unionist party among the miners. The evidence they gave is a fair test of their intelligence.—*Author's Note.*

issue of the struggle. The irritation increased daily, and serious disturbances occurred, in spite of the police. All colliery work was suspended. The men on strike succeeded in persuading the miners, who were called in to supply their place, to return home, and paid their travelling expenses. In order to obtain hands, the proprietors of the Gresley Wood and Swadlincote Collieries engaged special trains, which avoided the stations watched by the Unionists, and stopped in lonely spots, where the new comers alighted, and thence found their way by stealth to the mine. This measure was successful; the old workmen returned to their labour, and came out of the Union.

The Commission was sitting early in 1868. There had been several strikes already that year. One in January at Lord Vernon's works, on which occasion, after standing out a month, the men submitted to a reduction of wages. Another, also in resistance to a reduction, occurred in Lancashire. This was attended with disturbances more serious than any we have had to describe before. There are numerous coal and iron works in the district between the towns of Wigan and St. Helens, which is very rich in minerals. One mine alone, the Wigan Iron and Coal Company, employs 9,000 workmen, and produces annually 1,750,000 tons of coal. The price of coal having fallen, the directors of the Company determined to reduce wages 15 per cent. This step they considered so necessary, that they would have preferred closing the mines to giving it up. On this occasion again, the leaders of the Union, which was established in 1862, gave a proof of their sagacity by advising the workmen to submit to the reduction. One of them, Mr. Pickard, whom it was impossible that they should look upon with suspicion, as he had always been conspicuous for advocating strong measures, endeavoured in vain to show them how fatal would be the consequences of resistance. He was not listened to— the branch societies of Wigan and St. Helens rebelled against the central authority, and would not even hear of coming to terms. The more sensible among the men, who refused to go on strike, were annoyed in every possible manner, especially after they were joined by some strange workmen imported into the district. Notwithstanding all the efforts made by the leaders of the South Lancashire Association, the miners on strike, 1,500 in number, among whom Unionists and non-Unionists were mixed, seized the works of the Wigan Company, and remained in occupation of them several days. They would have destroyed all the machinery had it not been for the interference—so rarely called for in England—of the military. A detachment of forty soldiers and sixty policemen was one night attacked with stones near the Edge Green Colliery, and had much difficulty in dispersing the rioters. These disturbances were going on at the time the sittings of the Commission began, and both parties, each labouring under the excitement produced by this lamentable struggle, came and poured forth their complaints before it. The directors accused the men of acts of violence, and the leaders of the Unions of connivance with these acts; they also found fault with the patience—or, as they called it, weakness—of the magistrates charged with maintaining order. The Union leaders, on the other hand, declared that they used their utmost efforts, so far as even to endanger their influence, in endeavouring to enforce moderation and to calm the passions, which they reproached the directors with having provoked and irritated by their previous conduct. At any rate, this discussion clearly proves that none of the offences of which the workmen were guilty on this occasion, can be attributed to the influence of the Unions.

In spite of all these contests, the increase in miners' wages during the last forty years has not been at all in proportion to the increase in the price of all the necessaries of life, and, consequently, they are relatively worse off now than they were formerly. It is unjust, therefore, to blame the Unions for having endeavoured to increase the price of labour, if, as their advocates assert, these efforts have not been in vain, but have really contributed to obtain for the workman a better remuneration for his toil.

The pitmens' Unions are formed upon the same model as those we have previously described. The "National Association," founded at Leeds in 1863, consists of 35,000 members : it is simply an amalgamation of the branches established in the different districts, each of which raises its own fund, is governed by its own rules, and has the independent management of its own affairs. The subscription to the National Association is a penny a month only, and its functions are, by exercising a general direction over the efforts of the local branches, to insure united action in striving to get laws passed more favourable to the miner, to protect the rights and uphold the claims of every individual member, and finally, to obtain a reduction of the day's work, which, the Unions believe, ought to be limited to eight hours. The central society exercises only an indirect influence over strikes; the local branches decide upon them and bear the expenses. Nevertheless it occupies a very important place, and in proof of this, Mr. McDonald told the Commission that, during the seven years which he has spent as president—first of the Scotch Association, then of the National Association—he has attended 1,600 meetings, travelled 230,000 miles, and written 17,000 letters. The branch Unions singly are sometimes very powerful bodies. The South Yorkshire Association, which was founded in 1858, is subdivided into 48 branches, and consists of 7,000 members, who pay ten shillings admission money, and a weekly subscription of ninepence, or one shilling, according to circumstances. The Lancashire Association, established in 1862, is also composed of 7,000 members, paying ninepence a week. This society allows nine or ten shillings a week to workmen while on strike, and in addition insures its members 5*l*. or 6*l*. for funeral expenses.*

The proprietors, on their side, have sought to resist this new power, either by combining together, or by establishing associations of workmen under their own patronage and direction. We have shown the action of these combinations on all the important strikes which they have been formed to meet, and that their function is to ensure united support against attacks, and to lay under interdict, when necessary, the rival associations of the men, by denying such of them as belong to these access to the mines, and using their influence to prevent their obtaining any employment They have gone so far as to adopt the system of "black lists." A circular was produced before the Commission which had been sent round by the secretary of one of these associations to all the masters members of it, charging them on no account to employ any of the workmen named in it as Unionists. The mutual benefit societies which have been established by some masters among their men, with a view of coun-

---

* The Scotch Miners' Unions apply their funds to trade purposes (strikes) only.—*Author's Note.*

teracting the influence of the Unions, seem to be excellent and well-managed institutions; but the operatives have reason to complain that these are even more liable than the much-abused Unions to the charge of obtaining members by coercion. It is quite true that in some mines these societies are kept up not by voluntary subscriptions, but by a deduction imposed on all the men's wages, so that the workmen, who are either discharged or leave the mine of their own accord, lose all right to participate in the advantages secured to them by their paid-up subscriptions: and it is in the power of a director to aggravate the punishment of dismissal, by the indirect infliction of what may chance to be a heavy fine.*

It has been necessary, in order not to interrupt the history of strikes, to lose sight for the time of the unceasing efforts made by the Unions to obtain legal protection against the dangers to which the men are exposed in the mines. The hours of labour having been reduced, the employment of women and children underground having been forbidden, the miners' associations next had to devote all their attention to the measures indispensable for securing safety in coal-pits.

* We must not omit to mention a society, though one possessed of small influence, called "The Free Labour Registration Society," which is not limited to the mining trades. It is a kind of registry office, in which men out of employment may enter their names, and to which masters in want of hands may apply.—*Author's Note.*

The large number of victims to accidents, in spite of all the precautions taken to protect life, proves how necessary these precautions are. They accordingly engross the attention of both masters and men. Their efforts are, above all, directed against the explosion of fire-damp. The admirable invention of Sir Humphrey Davy, which consists in enveloping the miners' lamps with a covering of network impenetrable to inflammable gas, has much diminished danger, but has not entirely removed it. Miners will sometimes break open the sealed fastenings of their lamps in order to light them up again; or carry matches in their pockets; or the lamps have been known to ignite the gas either from being broken by a blow, or from their metallic network getting heated red hot. All measures, therefore, for securing safety ought to be both taken and kept up as strictly as if the Davy lamp did not exist.*

Strong ventilation is needed in order to keep constantly carrying off the noxious gas, but unceasing watchfulness is still more needed to guard against the imprudence of the workmen, and to prevent accidents, when the presence of gas is revealed. The masters, unwilling to submit to any control from the Unions, accuse them of being an obstacle to the exercise of this

---

* The great improvements known to have been effected in this lamp do not render it less necessary to take every precaution.—*Author's Note.*

watchfulness by developing a spirit of independence among the men. The miners reproach the masters with neglecting many essential precautions, and especially with frequently endangering life by relying too exclusively on the safety lamp.

The Unions, as has been told, succeeded in 1834 in having this question referred to a Parliamentary Committee. At their request it was taken up again in 1850, and, after an inquiry, presided over by Lord Wharncliffe, an Act, which, by the by, completely justified the complaints made by the associations, was passed, creating official inspectors specially charged with the duty of controlling the sanitary state of mines. But the limited number and restricted authority of these inspectors rendered their efforts insufficient. The Unions petitioned again; another committee was appointed in 1852, and again in 1853, and a more complete measure was passed in 1855. The workmen, however, were not yet satisfied; they said that the inspectors could not come and examine a mine at any moment, and that their visits were too rare to be of any real use. The representatives of the various Unions being convinced that the thoughtlessness and neglect of precaution shown by the miner, which are the cause of so many accidents, arose from his ignorance, proposed that a system of compulsory education should be established, and presented to Parliament a petition, with more than 50,000 signatures, offering that the expenses of carrying out this scheme should be met by a contribution imposed on their own wages, on the condition only that some of their body should be members of the governing council. A bill, in accordance with this proposal, was introduced by Sir George Cornewall Lewis, a wise and liberal statesman, whose loss is still felt in England. It met with strong opposition, and was called an attempt at exceptional legislation; the most important clauses were thrown out in the Commons, and only a few insignificant provisions facilitating the education of miners were preserved; the Unions, therefore, continued their importunities. The National Association of Miners was at this time engaged in urging upon Parliament the expediency of rescinding the "Master and Servant" law,* the repeal of which was called for by delegates from all the Trades' Unions. It succeeded in this; and at the same time in getting the subject of the inspection of mines and the education of miners again referred to a committee of the House of Commons. The report of this committee was very favourable to the proposals of the workmen, and the session of 1869 will not pass without legislation on this subject.

After what has gone before, it must be acknowledged that the Unions are not answerable for the worst acts of violence arising out of the demands for increase of wages,

* *See* above, p. 26.

and also that they are not entirely engrossed by this idea alone. They have made a point of showing, from the very first years of their existence, that they are well aware that they have a part to play besides that of supporting strikes, and duties to fulfil towards the working-classes who have entrusted them with the care of their interests. If, in the course of their stormy career, they have committed a few errors, have they not nobly redeemed them by their persevering efforts to improve the miner's condition?

CHAPTER VII.

THE IRON SHIP-BUILDING TRADE.

THE construction of iron vessels now occupies the first place in the shipbuilding trade of England.

The attention of the commissioners was, naturally, directed to this trade after their inquiry into the state of the factories in which the metal is manufactured, and of the mines which provide the coal with which it is melted.

The principal dockyards of the United Kingdom are those on the banks of the Thames, the Mersey, and the Clyde; in the outskirts of London—at Millwall, and the Isle of Dogs; at Liverpool, and Birkenhead; at Glasgow, and at Greenock. Frames built of wrought-iron, and sometimes of steel, and with an outer covering of sheet-iron, have, to the advantage of England, which is rich in iron but poor in timber, taken the place of the old-fashioned wooden vessels. The *Great Eastern*, and some of the finest ships of the English iron-clad fleet have come out of the Thames Iron Shipbuilding Company's yards; there, too, most of the second-rate navies of Europe are supplied; fineness of lines and solidity of construction distinguish the vessels turned out by the yards in the Isle of Dogs. The Messrs. Laird, whose works are on the banks of the Mersey, are unrivalled in England for their turretted ships of war. Ships built especially with a view to speed come from the banks of the Clyde: such are the celebrated liners of the Cunard Company, and their worthy rivals of the French Transatlantic Company; from the Clyde, too, started the famous blockade-runners, in which everything was sacrificed to speed, and which, in spite of the Federal cruisers, carried on so lucrative a trade with the slaveholding States during the late war in America. The English Government, though more and more in the habit of giving contracts to private firms, continues to employ a large number of workmen in its dockyards at Portsmouth, Devonport, and Chatham.

Work by the day is the system generally adopted in this trade, except on the Thames, where piecework is combined with it in almost all the yards. It is done in this way—a shipwright, who is a superior workman, undertakes a piece of work or job by contract, and then pays the workmen, whom he employs to perform it, by the day. Sometimes several workmen go partners in a contract for a certain job to be done at a price agreed on; as long as they are working at it, an instalment out of the contract money at the rate of so much per day is paid them at the end of every week, and when the job is finished they divide the remainder. Sometimes only a small number of workmen sign the contract, and they, like the shipwrights, pay the men, whom they employ to help them, by the day, reserving for themselves alone the division of the ultimate profits of the affair, and, agreeing also, if it should so turn out, to stand the loss. In either case it is the practice now for the workmen to rate themselves for the weekly instalments of pay, allowing one man five shillings, another five-and-sixpence, and a third six shillings, according to their respective merits.

After the workmen, who build the ships' frames, we come to those who complete them, such as carpenters, joiners, painters, &c. These generally make common cause with the workmen of the class first mentioned; but they possess their own special Unions, just as is the case in the various branches of the building trade, or else they belong to some one or other of the great associations, already noticed: it will not, therefore, be necessary to refer to them again.

As no considerable strikes have occurred in the dockyards on the Mersey, we may confine our attention to the establishments on the Thames and the Clyde. The history of these two bitterly rival trades, the one in the outskirts of London, the other at Greenock, is so entirely distinct, that it will be better to give a separate account of each.

In the London branch of the ship-building trade Unions have been in existence for a very long time. The "Shipbuilders' Provident Union of the Port of London" was established in 1824. At this period iron ships were almost unknown; but as they became more general and supplanted the old-fashioned structures, the men employed on the wooden vessels gradually took up the new trade. The unfair share of the profits which men who took a contract gained over those whom they engaged at daily wages, had long been the subject of constant dispute. The Union began by opposing this system, and endeavoured to enforce one by which all the workmen should share equally in the profits after a job was finished. In this it generally succeeded, and also in establishing the rule—after a hard struggle, accompanied by a strike in 1825—that the price in no contract should be fixed at a rate which would give less than six shillings a day per man as long as the work lasted. After these two points were carried, there was scarcely any subject of quarrel left,* and the funds of the

* The only case of strike after this, is one that occurred in 1856, and was confined to the yards belonging to the Messrs. Young. The men wanted to introduce an alteration in the distribution of the hours of labour. Messrs. Young opposed this, whereupon the men turned out, and after remaining four months on strike, and spending 3,000*l.*, obtained their object.—*Author's Note.*

Union accumulated so fast, that it was able to devote the greater part of them to the relief and assistance of the members. This society consists now of 1,400 members, and posesses a reserve fund of 12,400*l.*

The year 1851 was remarkable for a disastrous strike in a different branch of the shipbuilding trade. The joiners wanted the employers to adopt certain rules as to labour; the masters refused, and combined to resist the demands of the men. This could be done more easily at that time because the Unions were not then in such great force as they are now, in fact they played only a secondary part throughout this affair. The strike meanwhile spread rapidly all over the country. The workmen bore their sufferings, which lasted a long time and were most trying, with admirable firmness and temper. Mr. Samuda, a member of Parliament, and a great shipbuilder, who had himself joined the masters' combination on this occasion, in speaking of this strike before the Commission, uses the following words: "They (the workmen) exercised such an amount of courage, and they went through such an amount of endurance, that I do not hesitate to say that it was one of the most painful things a man could experience to be successful in such an undertaking." After three or four months the battle ended in the complete success of the masters; and the workmen were compelled to withdraw their demands, having exhausted all their resources.

Trades' Unions are almost as old an institution on the banks of the Clyde as on those of the Thames. The "Shipwrights' Society," of which Greenock is the head-quarters, was founded in 1828. Similar associations were subsequently established in the other branches of the trade. They rapidly took an extraordinary development; as long ago as in 1836 they had won so high a position in the town as to negotiate on equal terms with the great shipbuilders of Greenock. So much so that, on the 23rd of November 1836, the masters and the joiners signed a regular treaty, by which the latter undertook not to object to the number of workmen employed in the yards, nor to require them to become members of the society, provided all fresh hands had gone through a regular apprenticeship.

In 1839 most of the masters formed an alliance to resist the Shipwrights' Society, which was bound by no treaty with them, but, on the contrary, wanted to oblige them to employ none but workmen belonging to the Union. The masters gained a temporary success; but later on, in 1857, they were obliged formally to recognize the Union's right of interference in all their relations with their workmen. They had to apply to it when they were in want of hands, and to address their complaints to it if they were not supplied fast enough. The society often was purposely slow in furnishing men, in the hope that a scarcity of labour might cause a rise in wages; on such occasions the masters would represent that this proceeding would have no other effect than that of diminishing the work done in their yards. The Unions have sometimes demanded the discharge of a man for refusing to join their body, and have almost always succeeded in obtaining it.

This state of affairs lasted till 1866. The imprudence of the Unions then brought on a crisis, which was fatal to them. At this period the trade was in one of those moments of depression when employers, instead of having anything to fear from a strike, wish for one, and are only too glad to make any unreasonable demand of the workmen an excuse for stopping their works, which they are carrying on only at a loss. That was exactly what happened on this occasion: the workmen demanded shorter hours of labour without any corresponding reduction of wages. The masters proposed, in a conference held with the delegates of the different Unions, that they should work three hours a week less (fifty-seven hours instead of sixty), provided they would consent to an equivalent reduction in the day's wages. They could not come to any agreement, and some of the workmen struck. Immediately all, but three, of the shipbuilding firms combined and formed in a few days a most powerful Union under the name of the "Clyde Shipbuilders' and Engineers' Association." They closed all their shops, and gave notice that they would not open them until the men's demands had been withdrawn. This lock-out kept 18,000 men out of work for several months, and inflicted great suffering on them. At last they gave in, and have never since, with the exception of a few partial strikes, been able to make head against the Shipbuilders' Association. This society is more strongly organised than any of the employers' associations previously noticed, and its rules are quite as strict as those of the workmen's unions. It consists of thirty-five subscribers, each one of whom is bound by promissory-notes payable at sight, and lodged in a bank, to pay, whenever required, at the rate of four pounds for every man he employs. This secures the association a fund of 100,000*l*., on which it could draw at any time. One member cannot engage another's apprentices without the latter's consent. Lastly, they have consented to sacrifice their independence so far even as to agree that no member shall, during a strike, keep his works going without the consent of a majority of two-thirds of the society, and that he shall, when so ordered by the same majority, discharge all, or a part, of his workmen.

Sometimes the frames are made, neither by iron nor wooden shipwrights, but by men brought up to the general iron trade, especially the makers of steamboat boilers, which, being joined by rivets, are constructed in exactly the same manner as iron ships. These workmen form a class apart, and possess a powerful Union, which was founded in 1834, and consists of 7,000 members: it is subdivided into numerous branches, and its headquarters are at Liverpool. In spite of the large resources at its disposal, the numerous strikes in which it has been engaged have rarely been successful. In 1862 the members, being afraid of the old shipwrights' competition, and, therefore, not wishing to instruct them in the art of iron shipbuilding, refused to work with them. They went on strike, first at the Royal Dockyard at Chatham, afterwards at Messrs. Wigram's yard on the Thames; but, after a protracted resistance, were obliged to yield. Some of the men belonging to this Union—called the Boilermakers' and Iron Shipbuilders' Society of Great Britain and Ireland, in number about 2,000—found themselves involved involuntarily in the great Greenock fight of 1866, and thrown out of work by the stoppage of the works in the yards on the Clyde. Although their Union had always been opposed to the demands which provoked the lock-out on this occasion, nevertheless it suffered by it; for it could not refuse to come to the assistance of its members, who were thrown out of work in consequence of a quarrel in which they had taken no part, and their keep cost the society 2,000*l*. It was otherwise at Liverpool: there a branch committee, having decided upon a strike against the wishes of the central authority, received no support from it.

According to its original rules, this society offered all sorts of advantages to its members in the way of benefits; and, although it has not spent much money, in proportion to its income, on strikes, the fund raised by the annual subscription of 2*l*. 8*s*. for each member has not proved sufficient to meet the expenditure.*

Accordingly, out of 55,000*l*. raised in the course of six years, 1,000*l*. only remains as a reserve fund; and if it was bound to abide strictly by its rules, it would now be on the eve of inevitable bankruptcy. But as it was founded chiefly for the purpose of assisting such of its members as are out of work, it has always made both the amount of relief granted on any other account, and the amount of the subscription imposed, subordinate to carrying out this one object. Accordingly, at the time of the commercial panic, the subscription was raised from three shillings and sixpence to four shillings a month; and the allowance to members out of work was

---

* The expenditure for the six years previous, and up to January 1, 1868, is composed of the following items:—

		£
Expenditure for Sickness		18,145
,,	Funerals	4,213
,,	Medical attendance	5,052
,,	Travelling in search of employment	15,698
,,	Aged members at home	1,111
,,	Aged and superannuated members	1,391

—*Author's Note.*

reduced from one shilling and eightpence to one shilling a day.

These figures show in what a depressed state the ship-building trade now is in England. This is a point upon which both masters and workmen agree. Since the termination, in 1865, of the civil war in the United States, the famous blockade-runners—which, for the time, made the fortune of the Greenock yards—are no longer required; while the Thames iron shipbuilding, like many other branches of trade, led away by blind confidence in the great house of Overend, Gurney and Co., became entangled in the wild speculations of that company, and when it fell, was involved in its ruin. Mr. Samuda states that he was himself obliged to reduce the number of his workmen from 2,000 to 200; and that, out of all the yards which were in existence before the year 1851, his own is the only one which has not failed. One very remarkable fact is, that the English ship-builders are beginning to admit that their difficulties are added to by the increasing competition of France, who threatens to supplant them in the foreign market.

Each party accuses the other of being the cause of the present state of things, and there is a good deal of justice in the complaints of both. The masters reproach the workmen with demanding an increase of pay, which they cannot grant without ruin to themselves; the workmen justly complain of not being so well paid now as they were thirty years ago. It is quite true that the rise in wages has been even smaller in the dockyards than in the coal-pits; and, owing to the depreciation of money, a workman cannot with his ordinary weekly pay buy the same quantity of provisions and fuel that he formerly could. In London he earns more than at Greenock, but then everything is dearer there; and wherever wages have in appearance most risen, the rise has been more than balanced by other circumstances: thus fifteen years ago a riveter earned twenty-four shillings a week at Liverpool, he now earns twenty-eight; but then, fifteen years ago, he had to put in only about 700 rivets in a week, whereas now he has to put in 1,000. There must be a revival of trade before we can expect to see any sensible improvement in the condition of the workmen.

II. MACHINERY AND ENGINEERING.

Our account of the series of iron-working trades would be incomplete if we omitted to notice the manufacture of machinery and steam-engines. We therefore offer a short resumé of the information on this subject collected by the Commission, and scattered over the ten volumes of reports which it has published. The engineering trade is so important an element in the prosperity of our age that it may be said to feed with its products all other industries. It may be divided into four branches, viz., the construction, first, of steamships; second, of locomotive engines; third, of the admirable mechanical contrivances by which our factories are worked; and, lastly, of the perfect and wonderful tools without which none of the foregoing could be produced.

Manchester alone, out of the several centres of this great industry, occupied the attention of the Commission. There the Atlas works, which turn out eighty or a hundred locomotive engines a year, have their seat; there, too, are the great railway engine-works of Beyer and Peacock, and Whitworth and Company's establishment, celebrated for the production of cast-steel cannons, and still more for the precision of their instruments employed in working cold iron; and, lastly, the Bridgwater works, founded by Mr. Nasmyth, one of the most ingenious inventors of our time.

The men employed in these works are divided, as in other trades, into artisans,—that is to say, men of experience in their calling,—who are put to what is called skilled labour only; and labourers, who are supposed to be capable of such work only as requires mere muscular strength. The artisans, who have to serve five years as apprentices, make a great point, like their brethren in the building trade, of keeping up this despotic custom. They think that the monopoly thereby secured to them affords a protection against an undue increase of their numbers and against the fall of wages. They look upon it as an acquired right and a sort of property, which they refuse to share with intruders.

Some sorts of work, such as watching self-acting machinery, the production of which never varies, are paid by the day; others are paid by the piece or job. In this, as in the shipbuilding trade, one man will often take a contract for some important piece of work, such as setting up a locomotive engine, and will then engage the assistance of others, whom he pays by the day. But in such cases the Union exacts that the men so engaged shall all have a share in the ultimate profits of the undertaking in proportion to the wages of each. The Union, however, is not, on the whole, in favour of piecework, and we find the objections urged against the system by the masons and joiners repeated. The workmen are afraid of its exciting a spirit of rivalry among themselves, which would tend to bring down the rate of wages; and they assert that work thus paid is never so well done as that paid by the day. This last is a point upon which they are constantly insisting in their arguments with the employers.

A number of Unions existed among the engineers before the year 1851; but they were quite independent of one another, and though they often had to maintain partial strikes (one of which, that occurred at Manchester in 1837, was rather serious): these struggles always preserved an essentially local character. In 1851 all these societies united and became merged in one only, which includes in its ranks almost all the workmen belonging to the trade; this is the Amalgamated Society of Engineers, the most powerful probably of all the Unions in England, the organization of which we have already explained in our previous mention of it. Its opponents even acknowledge that it has always acted with forbearance and temper: the struggles in which it has been engaged have never been attended with any violence, however great the importance of the questions involved in them might be, and however severe might be the privations inflicted upon the workmen by strikes. Strikes, however, have been of rare occurrence; the most serious broke out in December 1851, a few months only after the formation of the society.

The system of apprenticeship was the excuse for it,[*] but its real cause was the introduction of machinery modifying the relations between production and labour. Constant partial strikes had given a great stimulus to the inventive genius of some of the great manufacturers. Tired of the perpetual struggle with a body of artisans, who became more exacting in their demands the

---

[*] The cause of the great strike of 1851 was a resolution to resist overtime and piecework. The apprenticeship question was not raised distinctly.—*Editor's Note.*

more they believed themselves, owing to their special knowledge, to be indispensable, they sought to find out machines which should be able to perform the same tasks as these skilled workmen, and the management of which could be learnt in a few days. Everyone in these days is acquainted with the instruments which perforate round, square, elliptical or conical holes in iron, which plane it, cut curves in it, saw it, bend it, in a word, turn it as if with a lathe, and copy the most varied patterns with wonderful accuracy. A child can manage several of them at the same time; a handle pulled backwards or forwards, a few drops of oil judiciously applied, are all the human aid required to set and to keep these obedient servants at work. No man has contributed in a greater degree to this astonishing revolution than Mr. Nasmyth. Beginning as a simple workman, he first distinguished himself by, what he calls, his Robinson Crusoe inventions; and he still shows with pride, as the foundation of his great fortune, a little oven, which he constructed for cooking his dinner, and by means of which he saved three shillings out of his weekly wages of fifteen shillings. The perfection of his machinery set him free from the necessity of employing only skilled mechanics; he put an end, in his own works, to the apprenticeship system, and placed his magnificent automaton machines in the hands of anyone who had intelligence enough to direct them.

In acting thus he was attacking strong prejudices and inveterate habits. But it must be owned that he was right in fighting for the productive principle. In fact the extreme division of labour, which is often a necessary consequence of the modern industrial system, would be fatal to the intellectual progress of our time, were it accompanied by the old traditions, by which a man, or sometimes even a family, was confined to one special line of business. Machinery diminishes the labour of the workman, and sets his hands free from the long apprenticeship which gave them special skill in a particular trade; he can then escape from the narrow bounds within which he was confined by his contracted bodily powers, and a wider field is thrown open to him, in which to exercise his faculties. The example of the United States proves that the development of industry in a people is promoted, not hindered, by this versatility. Instead of mere living machines it creates men, and prepares these men to become citizens. By removing useless and obsolete prejudices, it opens a more extended career to individual enterprise and energy. The life of the illustrious Abraham Lincoln is a striking proof of this. The wood-cutter of Illinois did not reach the presidential chair, which he so nobly filled, until after he had tried many trades and practised some of the most opposite professions. If his ambition had been confined to attaining eminence in a single line he would not have dropped the axe to become successively a boatman, a lawyer, an officer of volunteers, a postmaster, a legislator, and finally the chief magistrate of a free people; neither would he, when arrived at mature age, and in the midst of the incessant occupation in which his life was passed, have supplied by severe study the defects of his childhood's education; and history would have had one name less to add to the short list of good and great citizens.

But these machines, which take the hardest portion of a workman's labour off his hands, may at times cause him an injury to which he is keenly alive. The work of his arms is at his own disposal, that of the machines is not; if, then, the former is to a certain extent supplanted by the latter, it is often a pure loss to the workman. As long as this continues to be the case, and until he is allowed a fair share of the profits derived from the increased production consequent on machinery, he will naturally be inclined to oppose the development of its power and of its use, and will believe that by so doing he is defending his interests and his means of earning a living. It has been shown that the improvements in hammers and in rolling-mills have been a great benefit to the artisans of the iron trade, because they were paid by piecework, and the rate of their wages relatively to the value of the iron manufactured has not changed. But this has not been the case in the engineering trade;

in this, on the adoption of the self-acting tools, the manufacturers gave up the system of payment by piece-work, which had till then prevailed in all work requiring manual dexterity; the workmen, therefore, who had been so ill advised as to oppose it before, could not then claim to have it restored. The men entrusted with the management of the machines, each one of which performed the work of five or six artisans, were paid by the day; and Mr. Nasmyth naturally greatly reduced the number of the men whom he employed. Before long still further improvements enabled him to leave to one man the direction of two, three, four, or even five or six self-acting tools; he then took the opportunity of making a still further reduction in his working-staff, and set as many machines as possible going under the control of one man, allowing him only a shilling a week extra for every additional machine. "I do not mean to say," he says himself, "that the shilling was a fair measure of the benefit that I got, but it was satisfactory to him and to me, and he got the shilling a week for each additional machine he superintended without any undue exhaustion." . . . . "When you put him upon six machines his profits to you were 6*l.* a week?"—"Yes." "And he received twenty shillings?"—"I was very niggardly in giving him only twenty-one shillings a week, but it is quite possible to spoil a man like that by giving him too much at once. . . . . However, he was satisfied; I was the employer, and he was the employed, and we were dealing together to our perfect mutual satisfaction." But by this arrangement the share in the profits hitherto allotted to labour was considerably diminished, and it might be foreseen that the workmen would stoutly resist a system which deprived them of work without offering them any compensation.

In the year 1851 several manufacturers in the Manchester district were following the example set by Mr. Nasmyth. Nevertheless the experienced artisans retained in their hands several descriptions of work for which their skill was indispensable. The prosperous state of trade at this time enabled them to be exacting, and the Amalgamated Society of Engineers afforded them an increase of power which they lost no time in turning to account. They began with the firm of the Messrs. Platt of Oldham, from whom they asked the following concessions, viz., entire discontinuance of piecework in all branches of the trade; double wages for working overtime; and that the management of the new machines should be kept exclusively in the hands of artisans and articled apprentices. Their firm, which owns one of the largest factories in England, refused to accede, and demanded the support of the other employers. These immediately locked out all their mechanics, and gave notice that they would not resume work until the Messrs. Platt's men had withdrawn their demands; moreover, they made it a condition that the men should come out of the Union. Three thousand mechanics were thus thrown out of work, and the stoppage of their employment reduced double or treble that number of labourers to idleness. The former were supported out of the funds of the society, nine thousand members of which were still at work in various parts of the country; the latter were frequently relieved by charitable donations drawn from the same source. But at the end of three months, and after spending 40,000*l*., they were obliged to yield. A good many of the mechanics preferred emigrating to giving up their Union, and went to Sydney in Australia, where they set up a branch society. The rest, about two thousand in number, submitted and came out of the Union. But it soon recovered itself; its financial prosperity was restored by extraordinary contributions, and the number of members increased rapidly. On the masters withdrawing their prohibition, the workmen flocked in crowds to join its ranks, and a few years after its defeat the Amalgamated Society was stronger than ever. Since these events, which have taught it to be more cautious, it has been engaged in only three strikes, which occurred in 1855, in 1866, and in 1868.

The first of these (1855) was directed against the Atlas Works, for employing, as the Union thought, too many boys. It was of short duration, and had no very important objects in view, and was remarkable only for the publication of black lists on both sides. The owners of the works set the example by sending round a list containing the names of all the men on strike to the other employers, who were requested not to give these men work. The workmen retaliated by publishing the names of all those who had refused to join them in the dispute, with a notice that all members of the Society were forbidden to work with the men so refusing.

In March, 1866, the smiths employed in Messrs. Beyer and Peacock's foundry struck work, in order to obtain the discharge of a new foreman, Mr. S. Hall, towards whom, rightly or wrongly, they entertained strong objections. A portion only of these men belonged to the Amalgamated Society of Engineers; but Unionists and non-Unionists acted in concert, without any interference on the part of the society in the matter. The owners of the factory procured other workmen, whom, on account of the hostility of the people around, they were obliged to lodge on their own premises, and the works, which had been suspended, were set going again. The old workmen considering that, under these circumstances, it was useless to prolong the strike, asked to come to terms. After it had been settled that those among them, whose places had not been filled up, should be taken back, on the condition of withdrawing their objection to Hall, it turned out that, by this arrangement, there were only nine Unionist men among the old hands reinstated. The secretary of the Amalgamated Society, who arrived while these negotiations were in treaty, succeeded then in persuading the workmen to revoke their decision, and to insist upon all the old hands being received back. The owners met this by a lock-out, which, however, they kept up for ten days only. At the end of that time they decided upon giving in, and took back all the men in a body, at the same time discharging both the new-comers and the foreman who had been the origin of the quarrel.

In 1868, the mechanics at Blackburn, in Lancashire, struck against a reduction of wages, and the struggle was still going on while the Commission was sitting. We need not go into the history of the partial strikes in which some local branches have been engaged between 1861 and 1868. It would add nothing to the information which the events already detailed have given us concerning the intelligent and resolute body of men composing the class of engineers, either as regards their present condition, their opinions, or their future expectations.

CHAPTER VIII.

VARIOUS TRADES.

THE field of inquiry open to the Commission was so large that it was obliged to put a limit to its researches, and, on coming to the point which we have now reached, to confine them to some few trades which demanded its attention rather on account of the powerful organizations of the associations established by the workmen belonging to them, than on account of the importance of the strikes, in which they have been engaged. Indeed, as has been already shown, the importance of strikes is by no means in proportion to the strength of the Unions whence they emanated; and, accordingly, the Commission, bearing in mind that its duty was not to give a history of these contests, but to investigate the working of trade associations, has wisely passed over several of the strikes which in their time have attracted the largest share of public attention, by making the public suffer from their effects.

Such an one was that of the cabmen in London some ten years ago, which has lately been repeated in Paris, and that of the engine-drivers on the Brighton Railway in 1865. These drivers wanted to force the company to give up a scale of graduated salaries, which enabled it to give, at will, a sort of premium for good conduct to a certain number of them. They chose for their strike the day of the Epsom races; a time when thousands of passengers are crowding the stations, and fighting eagerly for the smallest corner. The traffic managers, though duly warned by the drivers of their intention, did not believe that it would be carried out; but, though taken unawares, they did not give in. They placed all the men they could find, who had the slightest knowledge of driving, on the engines, got up beside them to direct them, and managed so well that the momentary embarrassment was lost in the midst of the disorder, which is one of the traditional attributes, and for many people the chief charm, of that uproarious day. The graduated scale was retained.*

The Commission concluded its labours by devoting several sittings to the London tailors, the Birmingham glass-makers, and the London printers. To the infor-

---

* A similar strike in America, caused the suspension for eight whole days of the entire traffic on the Erie Railroad, one of the principal lines in the New World. It may be imagined what an amount of annoyance this suspension must have occasioned to the inhabitants of the district dependent on the railway.—*Author's Note.*

mation contained in its reports we shall add a few words on the important class of cotton-spinners.

I. THE TAILORS' TRADE.

Up to the year 1834 the journeymen tailors of London were paid by the day. There existed among them an institution called "houses of call," a relic of the ancient guilds. The workmen were divided into seventeen or eighteen small clubs, of from 100 to 800 members each, which met in some public-house. Those who were out of work had to repair there every evening, and answer to a roll-call. When a master tailor wanted to engage any hands, he applied at the public-house, and was supplied with the men whose names stood first on the list.

Genuine Unions were established in 1832. In 1834 the societies asked for an advance of one shilling in wages, and a reduction of two hours in the day's work; this would have given them seven shillings for ten hours' work, instead of six shillings for twelve hours. But after a strike which lasted several weeks, they were beaten, and forced to break up, bringing down with them in their fall the institution of "houses of call." Soon after this, however, the masters came to an understanding with the men for the adoption of a different system of wages. It was agreed that thenceforth payment should be by piecework, according to a tariff called the log-book, which was established on the old scale of six shillings for the day of twelve hours.

In 1858 the tailors made a fresh attempt to organise themselves, and founded two societies. That called the "Amalgamated Society of Operative Tailors" was formed, as its name implies, by the union of several previously existing associations. The "London Operative Tailors' Protective Association" was established on the 10th of November, 1865: it developed rapidly. Two years after, it consisted of more than 7000 members, and was divided into seventeen branches. Although organised mainly with a view to strikes, it allowed its members relief in sickness, and a sum for funeral expenses. It also pronounced loudly in favour of piecework. Most Unions are in the habit of concentrating all their influence on their own particular trade; but this society soon showed that it was actuated by a very different spirit. The London Operative Tailors' Protective Association, not satisfied with forming an alliance with the other societies of tailors in England, has joined the United Kingdom Alliance of Organised Trades, which is a strictly defensive confederation, intended to resist cases of lock-out; none of the great English Unions belong to it: it (the Tailors' Society) is also a branch of the Workmen's International League, and endeavours to combine its efforts with those of the tailors in Paris, Berlin, and America.

The result of these alliances has been hitherto confined to some trifling assistance sent, it seems, from London to Paris, in 1867. It is wholly out of their power at present to render any effectual services to the interests which they seek to protect. Their object is to have an understanding with workmen out of England, so that when there is a dispute between employers and employed, the former may not be able to fight the latter by having work done abroad, and thus use the labour of different countries against each other as opposing forces. But these alliances can offer no serious obstacle to the masters, as long as they can find, without going out of England, plenty of workmen, unconnected with Unions, ready to answer to their call, who will spare them the necessity of applying either to France or Germany for the execution of their orders.

In 1866, both the operative tailors' Unions demanded and obtained a rise in the rate of wages. Three masters only refused it, and their shops were immediately put under strike : these three were members of an Union of master-tailors recently formed, which, from a feeling of *esprit de corps*, thought it its duty to support them. The masters, who had come to an understanding with their people, did not hesitate to lock the men out in order to assist their colleagues to maintain pretensions which they had themselves just allowed to be unreasonable. But at the end of ten days a meeting was held in

St. James' Hall, at which the tariff or log was completely remodelled, and wages were raised fifteen per cent.

This good understanding unfortunately did not last long. In the month of January 1867, a fresh dispute arose, again with reference to the log; the men accused the masters of constantly and little by little deviating from it, and demanded that it should be made uniform throughout London; the masters, on the other hand, asserted that this demand was only a pretence for getting a fresh increase of wages. The two parties met several times in conference, but without any result; and on the 22nd of April, 1867, the men, assembled in the Alhambra, declared a strike against eighty-eight firms, and three thousand of them left their shops. Some emigrated. Most of them were thrown on the streets, and having nothing else to do organised a system of pickets, who watched the masters' shops in order to prevent them from obtaining recruits to supply their places. The masters thus attacked resolved to avail themselves of the most stringent powers with which the laws quoted in a previous chapter provided them. They were quite right to prosecute, and to get sentence passed in the police court on men proved to have used threats and violence to prevent their companions from going to work; but, not satisfied with this, they attacked the system of picketing even when practised in an inoffensive manner; and, merely for being concerned in organizing the system, they committed Mr. Druitt, the president of the London Operative Tailors Association, together with some members of the committee, for trial before the Central Criminal Court on a charge of conspiracy. On the defendants promising that the pickets should be removed, the case was adjourned: but the Union refused to ratify the engagement which they had made, and elected other leaders in their place. These, too, were summoned before the court, and the jury following the directions of the judge, adopted the masters' interpretation of the law. The legal point therefore was settled: the whole system of picketing, which till then had been practised without opposition, was condemned by law: this satisfied the masters, and at their request, no sentence was passed upon the prisoners. The Union was beaten, its funds were exhausted, thousands of its members forsook it, and the strike came to an end. The leaders of the Union, nevertheless, had neglected no means of defence; they even endeavoured to turn their enemies' weapons against themselves. They discovered that Messrs. Mitchell and Harris had addressed a circular to the other members of the Master Tailors' Association giving them notice not to employ certain Unionist workmen therein named. Upon this Mr. Druitt, acting under the advice of Sir John Coleridge, one of the most eminent counsel at the bar, summoned the president and secretary of the Masters' Association on the charge of conspiring to deprive the men, so pointed out, of the means of earning their living. On being refused the summons, they became convinced, rightly or wrongly, that the law had one measure for the rich man and another for the poor man; that the spirit of the old statutes, which established their inferiority in former times, still survived; and that what was forbidden to them was permitted to the masters; and this grievance was added to those for which they demanded redress from the Commission, or rather, through its intervention, from Parliament and public opinion.

II. THE GLASS-MAKERS.

The trade of glass-making, which is spread all over England, has its head-quarters at Birmingham, where there are no less than twenty-two factories. It is well known that especially skilful and experienced workmen are required in this business. They work in the shops in groups of four, technically called "chairs," in which each worker belongs to a particular class, successively passing up from one to another class, according to the degree of his skill. They have to work hard. From Monday to Friday in every week the labour never ceases day or night: two relays of men take turns at the furnace for six hours at a time, each set resting only while the other takes its place. Piecework payment is universally adopted in this trade. In some towns a very old custom, dating from long before the establishment of workmen's associations, limits the amount of work which may be performed in a day; the Unions, however, do not approve of this rule, and would rather it were done away with wherever it exists.

Owing to the small number of men employed in this trade (barely 2,000 in the whole of England), and to the long apprenticeship through which they have to pass, the glassmakers are a singularly united and jealous body. The smallest fluctuations in the market affect them immediately. If one or two firms reduce their staff, a certain number of men are thrown out of work without any possibility of finding it elsewhere. For some years past 130, on an average, have been constantly unemployed; for this reason they have always made a stand against the admission of too large a number of apprentices into the trade.

One of the principal objects of the "National Flint-Glassmakers' Friendly Society of the United Kingdom," founded in 1849, was to regulate the admission of apprentices, and to limit it to a fixed number,—an object for which the workmen had long been striving. Success, it might be supposed, would have been all the easier to this society, in that nearly all the glassmakers belonged to it, and that, consequently, it had no competition on the part of non-Unionists to contend against. It consists at present of more than 1,700 members, who pay, some a shilling, others one shilling and threepence a week, according to the class to which they belong. Although at first established as a purely "Trade Society" it soon took to employing a portion of its funds in the relief of sick members. But, though the subscription was higher than that in most other Unions, it was forced in a few years to reduce the rate of sick allowance;* it is now, thanks to this economy, in possession of a reserve fund of 9,000*l*. The head-office is at Birmingham; but there is a sub-committee to each district, and a special agent of the society attached to every factory.

In 1858 the society made a strong effort to induce the masters to consent that the number of apprentices, whose increase alarmed them, should be limited to an uniform rate in all the glass-works. It began by applying to two firms, who were asked to allow only one apprentice to three chairs, or twelve men. A protracted strike followed the refusal of this demand, and at the end of three months all the glass manufacturers of Birmingham made common cause and locked out their

---

* This, in the beginning, had been fixed at twelve shillings a week for the first thirteen weeks; ten shillings, for the next thirteen; eight, for the following twenty-six weeks; and six shillings for the twenty-six weeks after that. Members subscribing a shilling a week received only two-thirds of these respective sums. These payments have been reduced to nine shillings, seven and sixpence, six shillings, and four shillings respectively. Lastly, two shillings a week is allowed to men who have not been at work for a year and a half through sickness, and are therefore looked upon as permanently disabled.—*Author's Note.*

workmen. The struggle lasted three months longer, and ended in a compromise. The men gave in as to the number of apprentices; but at the same time obtained a far more important concession of principle from the masters, who agreed that the number then fixed, at the rate of one apprentice to every two chairs or eight men, should never thenceforward be exceeded. This agreement does not seem to have cramped the trade, since the supply of workmen continues to be greater than the demand for their labour: evidence was produced before the Commission proving even that it was not insisted upon by the Union, except to provide for cases in which experienced artisans were not compensated for the loss of time and the trouble caused them by the unskilfulness of the new hands. Having no competition on the part of non-Unionist workmen to contend against, the Union has become the natural medium between masters and men, and, when they have a vacancy, the employers apply to the Union to fill it. Thus, in spite of some trifling disputes, no serious contest has arisen to disturb the relations established between them, nor to shake the position gained by the association. Its influence has effected a considerable rise in the workmen's wages. The masters would fain attribute to this rise all the commercial difficulties under which they are now labouring. But the evidence collected by the Commission on this subject is so contradictory that it is impossible to say how far this opinion may be correct.

III. THE PRINTERS.

Owing to the education and intelligence which are necessary in their trade, and to the knowledge which they acquire in following it, the journeyman printers have everywhere been found in the van of the army of workmen fighting to break the fetters with which their class has been bound for ages. It is well known that France owes the expunging of the offence of combination from her criminal code to the firmness and moderation with which the printers of Paris conducted a strike, which at that time was illegal.

The London printers had for a long time previously entered on this course. They have always made great use of the right of association. From the very first masters and men have settled their disputes through the intervention of delegates appointed by either side. In 1810 these delegates settled a complete scale for the wages of compositors, who were thenceforward paid by piecework. This scale has continued in force up to the present time, with the exception of a slight modification introduced in 1866, in favour of a trifling advance, being the first that has been granted to the compositors for fifty-six years, in compensation for the increased price of living. Taking this, however, into consideration, they are still entitled to complain that for half a century their pecuniary position, far from improving, has rather grown worse. All but three or four of the London printing houses accept this scale as regulating all contracts between themselves and their workpeople; both masters and men hold it in as much respect as an Act of Parliament, and all their disputes turn only upon the interpretation to be given to it.

Yet its authority was not always thus uncontested. Some of the master-printers having attempted in 1816 to make some alteration in it, the workmen united to protest against the innovation. A certain number of their body was constituted a committee, whose duty it was to see that the scale was acted up to, and this, later on, developed into an Union.* Ten years afterwards their example was followed by others, and the two committees or societies were amalgamated in 1834. The newspaper-compositors had established an association, having the same object, in 1820. In the year 1844, all the Unions existing among the journeymen printers combined to form one body under the name of the Printers' National Association: but this confederation was unable to hold together, and three years afterwards, when it was dissolved, the London book-compositors, and those of the

---

* Not being constituted with any view to promote or assist strikes, this society was no infringement of the combination laws; simple associations have always been permitted to exist.—*Author's Note.*

newspapers, established two separate societies. Lastly, in 1853, these two again amalgamated and gave birth to the existing Union, which consists now of 3,300 members, paying subscriptions, which vary, according to the amount of their wages, from twopence to sixpence a week. Besides this, those who wished to secure assistance in sickness, subscribed, until 1863, to a special fund set aside for that purpose; but in this year, the subscriptions to it having been found to be insufficient, the provident fund was extinguished as a separate one, and merged in the general fund of the society, which, from that time forth, has maintained a certain number of beds in the London hospitals, and also pays for the medical attendance of all its members. In addition to this, with a laudable solicitude for their intellectual requirements, the Union has established a considerable library for the use of its members.* The society is governed by a council composed of twelve book-compo-

---

* All these expenses, however, it looks upon as subordinate to the main object of the society: this is to support members out of work, either in consequence of want of employment, or of a strike, or a lock-out, and to provide for all the expenses of their disputes with the masters. The relative importance of the various heads of expenditure may be seen in the following cash account, which includes the ten years from 1858 to 1868:—

	£	s.	d.
Receipts	25,105	0	0
Expenditure	23,543	12	4
Balance	1,561	7	8

[ITEMS

sitors and two newspaper-compositors, whose decisions, however, may always be reversed by a general meeting. The secretary keeps a register, which all the members out of work have to sign; those only, whose names are found in it, have a right to receive the allowance of ten shillings a week.

The disputes of the compositors with their employers have been the occasion of many partial strikes, and have caused several printing establishments to be shut up for a time, but not one of them has ever involved the whole trade in London. The workmen have always shown great forbearance in these contests, and have never laid themselves open to the charge of trying to intimidate those who did not belong to the Union. It was not till 1854 that the society was called upon to renew the effort first made in 1816, and interfered to see that the scale of prices was properly carried out; the care of this had till then been left to a committee composed

Items of Expenditure.

	£	s.	d.
Assistance to members out of work	9,836	10	0
Legal expenses	2,756	1	0
Travelling allowance	695	3	10
Committee expenses	1,432	3	7
Medical attendance	569	2	0
Library	891	8	0
Assistance to other trades	1,185	0	0
Salaries of officers	2,471	7	0
Miscellaneous expenses	3,706	16	11
Total	23,543	12	4

—*Author's Note.*

exclusively of masters. At its request both sides agreed to nominate a commission consisting of three masters and three workmen, to be called the Court of Arbitration, who were to settle all difficulties to which the proper interpretation of the scale might give rise. Unhappily, this institution did not last long, it broke down before the first important question submitted to its judgment. The question was this: it was stipulated in the scale that the compositors should be paid only once for the pages of permanent advertisements which appear regularly in the newspapers, as long as these pages remain entirely unaltered; but inasmuch as, in most papers, some fresh matter has to be inserted, on almost every issue, in the pages already prepared for publication, some of the master-printers wanted, in calculating the wages to be paid, to deduct from the pages thus re-arranged, all that had been previously set up. The workmen, on the other hand, maintained that the moment a page was re-touched, the compositors ought to be paid again for the whole of it. The Court of Arbitration, which was called upon to try the question, was divided in opinion, and the president decided against the workmen. They submitted provisionally to his finding, but refused to accept his decision as settling the law on the subject, on the plea that he was himself an interested party in the matter: and, on a similar case arising, they repudiated the precedent of the Court of Arbitration, and carried the case before a court of law. The Court of Exchequer decreed twice in their favour, once under a single judge, and again under the full court. The masters appealed to the Court of Error, a tribunal of appeal, in which all the fifteen judges take part. Eleven of them were present on this occasion, and gave judgment once more in favour of the workmen. The master-printers avoided the consequences of this decision by handing over the printing of the advertisements to men paid by the day; and from that time no one has resorted to a Court of Arbitration.

At last, in 1866, the compositors obtained an increase of wages after long and troublesome negotiations with the Master Printers' Association, which was founded in 1855, a short time after the establishment of the Court of Arbitration, and with the special object of defending the interests of the masters in that Court. The expenses of living in London rendered this increase absolutely necessary; but the master printers were alarmed lest it should cause the London trade to be overmatched in the competition with the provincial towns, and granted it only after strong remonstrance.

There are Unions similar to that of the compositors in the other branches of the trade. We need notice that of the pressmen only, whose labour is also paid by the piece, according to a scale agreed upon with the employers. This Society, which was founded in 1839, provides neither a sick nor a superannuation allowance, but insures its members, when they die, 20*l.* for funeral expenses. Its special object is to defend their interests in all disputes with the employers, and to support them when they are out of work. The members have to pay a subscription of one shilling a week, which has been reduced to sixpence since they have been above 500 in number. It has never been concerned in any serious strikes, but has frequently been engaged in local disputes with the masters with the view of diminishing the number of apprentices.

IV. THE COTTON-SPINNERS.

Cotton-spinning was not one of the trades into which the Commission was directed to inquire.* The trials

---

* It has confined itself to collecting on this subject, as well as on that of many other trades, written documents, which will no doubt be annexed to its report, or to speak more correctly, its reports; for, as we have already said, the Commissioners, as might have been expected, are divided in opinion as to the conclusions to be drawn from their protracted inquiry, and it is understood that the minority will present a separate report containing their views, which are believed to be more favourable to the Unions than those of the majority. Up to the present moment (February 1869), these interesting reports have not yet been printed. The evidence that has been collected, though no doubt very remarkable, will merely add a few strokes to a picture, the general effect of which it cannot alter. We have not, therefore, thought it necessary to wait for its publication, the date of which is uncertain, before offering to those who take an interest in the debates about to take place in Parliament on the subject of Trades' Unions, an essay, which may, we hope, be of assistance in following and understanding them.—*Author's Note.*

with which the hard-working population engaged in this trade has of late been visited, are in no way connected with strikes. The unheard-of hardships which overwhelmed them during the civil war in America are the talk of the world. It is well known with what patience they endured their sufferings, with what courage they persevered in their sympathy with the great cause of abolition, although the war undertaken in support of it was the source of all their misfortunes; and it is also known how much was done for their relief by a great national effort. The cotton trade in France, after passing through a crisis equally terrible, is now engaged in a painful struggle with difficulties from which England was spared; this state of things must awaken a lively interest in all those who have our national greatness at heart, and a glance at the present situation of the English cotton-spinners may teach them much. The generous effort made in their favour has left behind a wholesome impression; but if it had not been essentially a passing effort, it would have degenerated into a fatal school of corruption, both for those who received and for those who gave relief; the former would soon have come to look upon a life of idleness as a right, the latter would have held themselves entitled to servile gratitude. In fact, noble as charity is, the relations between man and man in a civilised country can be founded only on mutual esteem and identity of interests, and not on the giving and receiving of alms. These feelings, we hope, will become more and more general in the intercourse of mill-owners and masters with their workmen. We will now show, in a few words, the great progress already made in this direction.*

Every one who has visited the manufacturing towns, must have noticed the immense buildings in which thousands of men, and also of women and children, the slaves, and, at the same time, the masters of some of the most ingenious machines ever invented by the mind of man, transform the shapeless bales sent from America and India, into fabrics at once solid, soft, and light. Much, unfortunately, might be said upon the subject of this excessive employment of women and children, a system fatal to education, to morality, and to family feeling: but with this we are not now concerned. The work in these factories may be divided into three principal branches. That of the carding machines, which disentangle the cotton; that of the spinning jennies, furnished with hundreds of bobbins to twine the thread; and that of the looms that weave it. The two last operations absorb the greater number of the hands employed in the manufacture. The weaving is now

---

* We believe that we have drawn the few facts here put together from the most reliable sources. We shall quote as an authority, among others, a simple hardworking old man, Mr. Maudsley, Secretary of the Northern Counties Operative Cotton-Spinners' Association.—*Author's Note.*

almost exclusively in the hands of the women and children; while the management of the spinning jennies is mostly entrusted to men. Unions, consequently, are found only in this last branch of labour; the female weavers have set up none among themselves, but the names of a few women appear in the lists of the Cotton-Spinners' Societies.

All payments in this trade are now made by piecework, and since the adoption of that method neither masters nor workpeople have ever had any doubt of its advantages. The system of apprenticeship is unknown.

The cotton-spinners began to form secret societies in 1824, but the repeal of the combination laws soon enabled them to act openly. It was about this time that, thanks to Arkwright's greatly improved machinery, the trade began to advance with rapid strides in the new course, which has led it to such abundant prosperity. The public, who paid less for cotton goods, and the manufacturer who produced them with less trouble, were alike enriched by this change. The working cotton-spinners alone did not profit by it, their wages remained stationary, and their position grew worse rather than better. Crowded together in badly-ventilated workrooms, subjected, even the women and children, to working hours whose length depended solely on the masters' will,*

---

* Some of the factories were kept going night and day.—*Author's Note.*

they had, in addition, to submit to strict arbitrary rules, to frequent fines; and, lastly, to the iniquitous truck-shop system. As might be expected, they availed themselves of the right of combining, in order to strengthen their Unions and to improve their position. Accordingly, the trade in Lancashire was constantly disturbed by strikes and lock-out. Gradually, however, abuses disappeared, they were either abandoned by the masters on a clearer discernment of their duties and of their real interests, or they were condemned by the Legislature. Wages were raised, and paid no more by the day but by piecework; the law interfered to abolish truck-shops, and also prohibited the employment of children unless they attended school; and, lastly, Parliament, by the Factories Act, limited the day's work to ten hours. Gradually, as these improvements were carried out, the spirit of hostility, by which the workmen had been so long animated against the heads of manufacturing establishments, vanished, and gave place to the confidence and mutual respect which became apparent in the great crisis of 1862.

The Unions, nevertheless, continued to take measures to increase their strength, and in 1853 the various societies then existing in the four counties of Lancashire, Cheshire, Yorkshire, and Derbyshire formed an alliance, and established the Equitable Association of Cotton-Spinners.

When all the spinning factories were paralysed by the scarcity of cotton during the war in America, the different associations formed among the workmen, both Trades' Unions and mutual benefit societies, disappeared, and their funds were rapidly swallowed up in the universal misery prevailing. But they came to life again as soon as the crisis was over, and sprung up with such vigour that the Spinners' Association, which consisted of 4,000 members in 1857, now numbers 8,000, that is, more than two-thirds of all the workmen belonging to the trade in the districts where the Union is established. The association was thoroughly remodelled in 1868. It is now managed by a council of delegates (each one of whom represents 200 members), and by an executive committee. Acting strictly as a confederation only, it allows the utmost independence to the thirty-six branches which compose it. Each one of these possesses its own fund, and has the choice of devoting it either exclusively to trade expenses, or of employing a portion of it in providing sick and superannuation allowance. The subscription to the central association is only a farthing a week. It grants no relief to members beyond a bonus, varying from 30*l.* to 50*l.*, to such of them as meet with accidents in the factory. But it has authority to decide upon the rate at which assistance shall be given in cases of strike or lock-out, and this has accordingly been fixed at ten shillings a week for the upper workmen, and at four shillings, two shillings, and one shilling for the helpers. Two very important powers are reserved to it, one, that of imposing on the whole confederation a rate in aid of any branch unable to meet its engagements; the other, that of refusing to sanction any strike which it holds to be not sufficiently justified. Thanks to this power, it has often succeeded in settling matters of dispute between masters and workmen by negotiation, and in so stopping a threatened strike. The strikes that it has not been able to prevent are few, and may be shortly reckoned. There was one at Preston and at Wigan in 1853, followed by a lock-out; another the same year, and again in 1867, at Stockport;* lastly, one which occurred in November 1868, and was directed against a cotton manufacturer of Cheshire, for refusing to recognise the Union. All these strikes were unattended by any violence; and most fortunately no really hostile feeling has ever interposed to counteract the memories of 1862. On the contrary, the masters and workmen of almost all the manufacturing towns have been in the habit of late years of meeting in conferences, at which they have jointly settled the rates of wages. Accepted by both sides as law, these rates are raised or lowered according as the state of the market allows the augmentation or

---

* This strike, which was more serious than any of the others, ended in the success of the men, but it cost them 4,000*l.*—*Author's Note.*

compels the diminution of the price of labour. The principal objects which the association has in view are to obtain the adoption of these rates, wherever they are not already in use, to see that all their conditions are carried out, and to observe the price-current of raw and manufactured material, in order to seize the moment for asking an increase of wages, and to avoid resisting a necessary reduction. It undertakes, also, to see that the law limiting the day's work in factories to ten hours is duly observed, and also to get that limit reduced, if possible, to eight hours, a reduction to which the workmen of almost all trades attach great importance, as a security for their independence and intellectual advancement.

By endeavouring to regulate their proceedings according to the state of trade for the time being, Trade Unions refute one of the accusations which have been most constantly brought against them. By means of a very complete register, in which all the fluctuations of the market are noted, the secretary has it in his power always to check any allegations of the masters and any demands of the workmen. The Unions, as caste prejudices are shaken off, and strikes are less frequently resorted to, see that they have a nobler part to play, and the influence of this happy change becomes apparent in the tone which they adopt in their intercourse with employers. Accordingly in a letter addressed, at the time of the strike in 1867, to the cotton-spinners of Stockport, who wanted to lower wages, the Union bases its arguments on the ground of the welfare of the community in general. "War and financial panics," they said, "have paralysed our export trade. This is a time not for increasing production, and seeking in vain, by lowering wages, to open out a market already glutted; but on the contrary one for reducing production. You had much better put the shops on half-time." We need not inquire whether this was the best advice that could be given under the circumstances; but this letter, in our opinion, certainly shows the new spirit which moves the workmen in some trades, and the nature of the influence exercised by their great associations, when these are well directed.

There is an immense difference between the sensible and thoughtful language of the Stockport Unionists and the absurd laws by which some societies have asserted their pretensions to rule trade according to their fancy, or the prohibitions intended to isolate one district from another. It is clear that Unions differ so much from one another, that it is not fair to include the whole body in charges to which only some of them are liable. We will conclude by a remark, which holds out encouragement for the future: in proportion as these societies spread and increase in strength, they become temperate and forbearing in their conduct. They are often animated by an intolerant spirit, when they are few and isolated, but as they gain power, they awaken to the responsibility of their position; the electoral system, by which they are governed, is almost always sure to bring out deserving men as their leaders, and the majority of the working classes has the good sense to listen to and to follow these, although they do not allow themselves to be used as instruments for flattering prejudices and gratifying passions.

CHAPTER IX.

THE REMEDY FOR STRIKES.

WE have shown how Unions came to be established, and the form they took; we have also shown their character and development, and the use which they have made of their power. We have put before the reader, as faithfully as we could, all that can help him to form a judgment on them. We will now sum up in a few words the chief heads of accusation brought against them, and the most conclusive arguments which they made use of in reply.

An impartial examination has dispersed the cruel and unjust suspicions which the Sheffield outrages fixed upon the whole body of Unions. There were men wicked enough to perpetrate these abominable deeds, and then to pretend that they were thereby serving the associations of which they were members; but the crimes of these men ought not to be laid to the charge of Unions in general. They are no more responsible for them than the chiefs of the League formerly were for the murder of Henry IV., or the Confederate generals for the assassination of President Lincoln.

They have been reproached with numerous acts of violence ; they have been accused of organising a system of intimidation against all who opposed them, and in a certain number of cases this has been proved before the Commission to have been true. This number, however, will appear trifling, if we take into consideration the enormous population from which examples might be selected, and the examples themselves show that workmen's associations require to be more enlightened and sometimes better managed, but certainly not that they deserve sweeping condemnation. Besides, if they are to be condemned, sentence will have to be passed upon the whole working-class in general, and not upon Unions in particular; for, along with the guilty acts attributed to their influence, at least as many more may be cited with which they have had nothing to do.

The censures which have been passed upon them from an economical point of view seem, at first sight, to be better justified, but on a closer examination they lose a great part of their force.

No doubt the spirit of monopoly and exclusiveness has to a certain extent been revived among them, but this has been kept up chiefly by the ruinous struggles against employers in which they have been engaged.

They have been accused as a body of wanting to restore the ancient guilds by limiting the number of recruits admitted in each trade, and by subjecting them to a long apprenticeship. But they found this system sanctioned by the usage of centuries; and in maintaining it they have merely yielded to the natural instinct of man, who does not like to see his younger rivals freed from the control to which he had himself to submit in his time; but they have never attempted to introduce it where it did not exist before.

Some Unions have wished to fix a limit to the amount of work that each man is to be allowed to perform, and, by establishing uniformity of wages, to bring all down to one dead level of mediocrity. But these are few in number, and the opinion of members of their own class, enlightened by argument, has persuaded many of them to abandon such ideas. The spirit of emulation, and the ambition to achieve results, with which every man conscious of intellectual power is inspired, have not been extinguished by Trades' Unions. Many of the masters examined by the Commission are themselves living proofs of this fact: for a great number of those among them, who are self-made men, were members of Unions while they were workmen.

The charge most frequently brought against these societies is founded upon the great number of strikes in which they have been concerned. This is the same as saying that the invention of gunpowder is the cause of all wars. By introducing more skilful management in the conduct of these struggles they have certainly increased their importance, but they have not made them much more frequent. They have occasionally, in their efforts to obtain their proper position, exceeded the limits of their legitimate influence; but, this position once secured, there is nothing to prevent their one day becoming both a new element of productive power and an earnest pledge of peace: some of their leaders are already looking forward to this happy accomplishment of their desires.

With respect to piecework, we have seen that, far from being condemned, it is preferred by almost every one of the trades which formed the subject of the Commission's inquiries. There are only two exceptions —the building and the engineering trades. And it must be remembered, as to the majority of the branches of the building trade, that the principal contractors agreed with the Unions in pronouncing in favour of payment by the day; indeed it is admitted that very often this is the only possible system of wages. "How can it be so bad," was the clever remark made by a witness in the course of his examination, "when, from the first Minister of the Crown down to the smallest boy in the navy, all Government servants are paid by the day, and do not perform their duties the worse for it?"

Whatever may be the various opinions on the subject of Trades' Unions, their existence is a fact: they cannot be put down; they are powerful, and their strength is increasing every day. What is to be their future? This is the question which everyone is now asking himself, and rightly, with mingled uneasiness and hope. This power, if ill directed, may increase to a most serious extent the inevitable confusion into which trade has been thrown by its mere presence. But, on the other hand, may it not, as we have suggested, possibly exercise a salutary influence? May not an effectual security be provided, by means of these associations, against the return of the trade contests, which resemble nothing so much as a Japanese duel, in which each combatant is obliged to put himself to death with his own hand?

We believe it may, and that the Commission has thrown a very encouraging light on this question.

We shall not stop to consider what advice the Commission is likely to give to Parliament, nor what laws are likely to be enacted. Whatever they may be, these laws will, we hope, add another stone to the edifice of English liberty. The Unions, at any rate, will be delivered from the false position which they now occupy, and a permanent measure will be substituted for Mr. Russell Gurney's temporary bill; but it is impossible to foresee as yet whether the party in the House which is favourable to Unions, or that which wishes to diminish their power, will eventually triumph. Will the first obtain for them all the guarantees which they desire, among others the suppression of prosecutions for conspiracy, the right of registration, which would establish them as corporate bodies, and the protection of their funds against a dishonest treasurer?* Or will the alarms of the opposite party prevail in Parliament? and will the associations be compelled to divide their funds into two separate parts: one to be employed in trade (strike) purposes only; the other in affording relief to the sick and aged members, without any power of drawing upon either in aid of the other? The decision to which Parliament may come, is, no doubt, a question of great importance, but it cannot control the future. From experience alone, not from legislation, can the societies learn the important part which they ought to aspire to play. As the experience of one nation may be of use to another, we will conclude by collecting out of the evidence produced before the Royal Commission the examples which prove that the existing Unions may either tend to promote harmony between employers and employed, or else, under favourable circumstances, may

---

* Sir Fowell Buxton introduced last year, a bill securing all these guarantees to Unions: unfortunately he has lost his seat, and will not be able to defend it in the new House.—*Author's Note.*

easily be made to give way to associations more capable of arriving at this happy result. That England has it in her power, already, to point to some such examples is entirely owing to the efforts of a few practical and enterprising spirits; the Commission examined three of these bold innovators, who have been particularly successful in the work of reconciliation.

The outline, which we are about to give, is in great part extracted from the evidence of Mr. Kettle, Judge of the Worcestershire County Courts; of Mr. Mundella, a manufacturer at Nottingham, and a member of Parliament; and of Mr. Briggs, a proprietor of coal-pits near Normanton.

I. ARBITRATION.

Mr. Kettle.

In consequence of the frequent occurrence of strikes, recourse has often been had to arbitration, and when it has been judiciously administered, the system has been productive of the happiest results.

In 1864 the contractors in the building trade and the carpenters not being able to agree, called in Mr. Kettle to settle their differences. Six masters and six workmen met as delegates, with Mr. Kettle in the chair. After a warm debate, in the course of which each side was heard, they ended by agreeing so well upon all the disputed points, that the chairman was not once called upon to give his casting vote. Encouraged by so successful an experiment, Mr. Kettle resolved to develop this meeting of referees into a permanent institution: the masters on the one side, on the other the carpenters, plasterers, and after a time the bricklayers, came into his views, and their plenipotentiaries, under his direction, composed a set of rules regulating wages, which, it was settled, should remain in force for a year. All the masters who were represented at this conference were bound to have these rules posted up in their workshops, and to give a copy of them to every workman they engaged, explaining to him that they formed the terms of the contract between them. It was provided by one of the rules that all matters in dispute should be referred to a meeting of six masters and six workmen sitting as a court of arbitration.* This court derived all its power and influence from the fact that it was composed, not of mere delegates, but of real representatives: the members of it, therefore, were competent to decide all questions brought before them, without having to refer them to their constituents, who, on their part, were bound to submit to its decrees. In short, both masters and workmen having pledged themselves to abide by the decisions arrived at under the rules, the English law

* Insignificant quarrels might be referred, in the first instance, to two members of the court, in order to avoid calling it together too often; but if either of the disputants declined to accept their decision, an appeal lay to the full court.—*Author's Note.*

invested these decisions with legal authority; and, in case of resistance, they could be made a rule of court and enforced by the county magistrates.

When once the rate of wages was by mutual consent unchangeably settled for a whole year, individual masters and workmen were bound only to adhere to the amount agreed upon, and all contracts, by which one party engaged to work and the other to find employment, might always be set aside in twenty-four hours, if either were dissatisfied. The price of labour being settled at the commencement of the building season, the contractors were able to make their estimates in perfect security, whilst the workmen ran no risk of finding themselves suddenly in reduced circumstances in consequence of a reduction of wages. The authority of the court of arbitration lasted for one year; at the end of the year its powers had to be renewed, the rules were again brought under discussion, and everyone was at liberty either to refuse or accept them. If, in the course of a year, a master wanted at the end of any week to pay his workmen less than the settled amount, they could appeal to arbitration, and enforce the award by summoning their master before a court of law on the charge of breaking his contract. No doubt they would have no right to prosecute him, if, even in the course of the year, he gave notice beforehand that he declined henceforth to accept the rules, and had them taken off the walls of the workshop; but then he would have been considered as going himself on strike, and if the other masters continued to give better wages than he offered, all his workmen would soon have left him. A violation of the rules by all the masters at once, acting in concert, would be a breach of honour of which it would be impossible to suppose them capable : on the contrary they have always submitted to the award. Mr. Kettle was called upon to establish an arbitration court at Coventry, and to preside over it; the court there was equally divided on the subject of the rate of wages, and Mr. Kettle, therefore, had to give the casting vote. He gave it in favour of the workmen, and the masters submitted to his decision without a murmur. In thus settling a rate of wages to prevail for a fixed period, whatever may be the fluctuations in the price of labour elsewhere in the meantime, masters and men are simply entering into a time bargain, and are morally just as much bound to stand by it, as any other vendors and purchasers in bargains of this nature.

Some members of the Commission seemed to think that practically it would be found that the workmen would not hold themselves as strictly bound as the masters to observe the rules. Without doubt a workman, who thinks he has a chance of getting better paid in another town, can always leave that in which the rate of wages seems to him insufficient. This, however, is by no means so easy a matter for him as it may at first sight appear to be; the removal of himself and his family and the change in all his habits, are considerations which will make him hesitate for a long time. But, it is then suggested, what hinders him from requiring an advance in wages the moment his legal engagement of twenty-four hours has expired? Why do not several hundred workmen combine together to make this demand? There is no law forbidding it, and when a responsibility is divided among a number of persons, each individual feels himself but slightly bound by his share in the moral obligations imposed by it. There would be no answer to this objection, did not the Union, appearing in a new part, and under a changed aspect, here interpose, and assume the responsibility repudiated by individuals. Although the representatives of the workmen are elected by non-Unionists as well as Unionists, they are always chosen from among the Union leaders, and act specially under its influence: all matters of business are transacted between the chairman of the court of arbitration and the secretaries of the association of masters, and that of the workmen. If the Union becomes a party to an agreement for settling the rate of wages, it is bound in honour to enforce the observance of the compact, and, being able to punish any of its members by fine or expulsion, it, and it alone, possesses the power of obliging them to respect it. In the development of association, Mr. Kettle's system will find exactly the securities of which it most stands in need. His success was so great at Wolverhampton, that he was soon called for to establish arbitration at Coventry and at Worcester, and the example so set was before long followed at Walsall, and in the Staffordshire potteries. Everywhere the results have been most satisfactory.

Mr. Mundella.

The arbitration courts, established in the hosiery trade at Nottingham by Mr. Mundella, present a still more perfect and remarkable example of their good influence on the relations between masters and men. They have restored peace and concord in the trade, which had previously been disturbed by the bitterest contests. It will be remembered that the town of Nottingham acquired an unfortunate celebrity at the beginning of this century by the riots and crimes of which it was the constant scene. The sanguinary measures adopted to suppress the Luddites did not succeed in putting down the passions under which those unfortunate people acted; and from 1825 to 1860 strikes were incessant. Mr. Mundella gives an exact description of the situation in the following passage, extracted from his evidence: "In times of depression a manufacturer pressed down the workman as low as he possibly could; and the less conscience he had, of course the more he pressed down the workman; and when the time for an advance came, or better trade, although the natural state of things,—that is to say, the natural demand for labour,—would sometimes force up wages a little, yet it was always resisted as much as possible. The men sent deputations from Trades' Unions round to the hosiers' warehouses. At one warehouse they would be told to walk downstairs. At another they would be told, 'Well, we shall wait till we see what our neighbours do.' After going round the different firms, and being received in that way, the chances are that the men would go home and strike; and it would depend upon circumstances how long they could keep out. They would perhaps ask for more than the trade could fairly give. It was simply starving out the manufacturer or the workman, till a compromise was effected." *

In 1860 affairs were at the worst; one class of work-

---

* Mr. Mundella, who appeared as a witness before the Commission, of which Mr. Roebuck is a member, and who was examined by him, was destined to meet the latter a few months later, upon the hustings at Sheffield during the late election, on which occasion he stood against Mr. Roebuck. Owing to the great and deserved popularity which Mr. Mundella has gained by his efforts to promote arbitration, the late Nottingham workman beat the learned counsel, who had so long represented the town of Sheffield. His reputation, experience, and impartiality, will make him a valuable addition to the House of Commons.—*Author's Note.*

men, after asking for a large increase of wages, had been eleven weeks on strike; they were supported by all the Unions; and the masters were on the point of resorting to the extreme measure of a general lock-out. " We knew," to quote Mr. Mundella again, " what this meant; it meant throwing the population on the streets, and we should have had a dreadful sate of commotion. We were sick of it, and some of us thought that better means might be adopted."

Inspired by a vague remembrance of the "*conseils de prud'hommes,*" Mr. Mundella thought of establishing a board of arbitration; and, with the assistance of two other masters, invited the workmen to a conference. They deputed twelve of their body, chosen from among the leaders of the Unions. The meeting was held, and at first each side looked very suspiciously at the other, like the envoys of two contending armies; soon the stiffness wore off; after discussing matters, they ended by understanding each other, and in three days' time, although the mutual prejudices on neither side were entirely removed, the outline of the new system was settled. All the masters of Nottingham were invited to meet together and elect nine delegates; about half of them attended. The workmen showed greater willingness. Those who had joined in the conference with Mr. Mundella, summoned general meetings of the Unions to which they respectively belonged, at which they reported the proposed plan to them, and persuaded them to adopt it. From that time forth its success was certain. The men outside these associations were few in number; they followed the suggestions coming from that quarter, and it is entirely owing to the powerful influence of the Unions that the arbitration boards were established, and enabled to act. Mr. Mundella goes as far as to declare that without them it would have been much more difficult to introduce arbitration boards, for that they could not have derived from any other source a support equal to that which the sanction of the working men's societies affords them. Simply by means of a good understanding between employers and employed, the societies, so lately absorbed in strife, were transformed into peacemakers. When nine delegates had to be appointed to represent the workmen, the machinery for their election was found ready in the organization of the Unions. The secretaries of the different societies in every branch of the trade collected the votes of all the workmen, Unionists and non-Unionists, and, by the suffrages of both, the most active Union leaders were elected to seats at the board. The alarm which their election might have inspired in some of the masters, who had been in the habit of looking upon their new colleagues as bitter enemies, was quickly dispelled. They soon came to acknowledge that they could not have found more sensible or more temperate mediators between themselves and the body of their workpeople. Ignorance and suspicion were still very prevalent; but these men, as the recognised leaders of their class, were frequently able to soothe its excitement, and to set its true interests clearly before it, without forfeiting its confidence, as their constant re-election proves: they never failed to exert the influence which their high position in the association gave them in favour of peace and justice.

The board, which was composed at first of nine, afterwards of ten masters, and of the same number of workmen,* naturally chose Mr. Mundella for its chairman, who for eight years has fulfilled the duties with the strictest impartiality. During this time his system has won a complete triumph over the open or concealed hostility with which his first efforts were met. Forty-two employers out of forty-five have recognized the authority of the board, and have formed a society to support it; and the ten workmen's delegates, who are now elected by the whole trade, represent more than 20,000 men. The board settles a scale of wages, which

---

* A committee, composed of four members, was appointed to arrange the business to be brought before the board, to settle questions of minor importance, and to decide when it should be necessary to summon extraordinary meetings. Two paid secretaries attend, and take minutes of the proceedings at the sittings of the board, one on behalf of the Masters' Association, the other on behalf of the Unions.—*Author's Note.*

are all paid by piecework: this scale remains in force as long as the state of the market allows it, and if any change in prices makes a modification of it necessary, the party requiring this must give the board a month's previous notice of the claim. These changes are now always settled in an amicable way; for when masters and men find themselves sitting, without distinction, round the same table, discussing their respective interests in a trade by which both earn their living, they soon learn that these interests are identical. More than once the workmen have withdrawn a demand for an increase of pay, to which they believed themselves really entitled, on the masters proving to them by figures that foreign competition made it impossible to grant it without losing a market for their produce. And in order further to convince them, the employers have frequently sent some of the working-men, who were their colleagues at the board, to visit France and Germany. The masters, on their side, in their discussions with the men, have been led to a juster appreciation of the conditions of labour; and on the representations of the latter, have decided upon never requiring them, even when trade is most brisk, to work more than ten hours a day. The harmony established between them is so complete, that for four years not a single resolution of the board has required to be put to the vote.

The system has the advantage of affording equal

protection to both parties. Every master knows that now no rival house can undersell him by an undue reduction of wages, and can, therefore, commit himself without apprehension to more constant and regular production. The workmen, instead of addressing all demands relative to wages directly to the employers, with the chance of having to support them by a ruinous strike, appeal to the board, and are sure of obtaining a just settlement.

Although its awards cannot, like those under the arbitration system established by Mr. Kettle, be made a rule of court, nevertheless they have all the force of law. Any workmen resisting them, as has once or twice happened, would be disowned by the Union, and refused all assistance, and would, therefore, not be able to hold out long. Those masters who have not openly recognised the authority of the board are, nevertheless, obliged practically to submit to its decisions. For if one of these offered his workmen wages below the rate adopted by the other manufacturers, the latter, instead of, as formerly, coming to his assistance and believing themselves bound to do the same, take side with the workmen, and reduce him to helplessness by finding employment for the men who have left him on account of the unreasonable reduction. So that, in fact, masters and men, united by a common interest, form one association, which is enlightened by the discussions and governed by the decisions of the board. To it are owing the most important improvements which have been effected in the condition of the working-classes. To it they are principally indebted for the strict observance, instead of, as before, the open evasion of the law for the suppression of truck-shops, with all their train of abuses. They owe to it, also, the uprooting of many prejudices, such as hostility against machinery, which caused the Luddites to take up arms, and the fatal consequences of which recoiled principally upon their own heads. The workmen's Unions which formerly in this business were purely "trade societies," and raised no benefit fund, have now hardly any expenses whatever to meet. At the same time that they preserve their power and their organization, they no longer, thanks to the cessation of strikes, have to make heavy calls on the purses of their members: the trifling subscription of a shilling a year suffices for all their needs. The fruitless struggles between capital and labour, which always ended by the public paying the cost, have thus disappeared from one of their most active centres; whilst the happy change has given no blow to healthy competition, which alone is really profitable to the consumer.

Such an example was sure to be imitated. In June, 1868, at the request of the workmen, a board of arbitration was established in the lace manufacture at Nottingham. The very day after that on which the Commission had been considering this subject, Lord Elcho, one of its members, had a meeting at his house between two, till then, bitter opponents : Mr. Lancaster, representing a number of colliery proprietors in South Lancashire, and Mr. Pickard, a leading man among the miners' Unions in that district. The three, assisted by Mr. Mundella's experience, arranged between them the outline of a board similar to the one at Nottingham. The men in the mining districts of Staffordshire, Middlesborough, and Cleveland, and even the workmen belonging to the building trade at Bradford, hitherto so unmanageable, have requested Mr. Mundella to come and provide them with the system which, under his auspices, has succeeded so well. And, what is still more remarkable, he has received a similar invitation from the Sheffield file-makers, in whose trade, as we know, the most violent means have been employed by the Unions to enforce their dominion.

II. Co-operation.

We have said enough to show that arbitration boards have succeeded in allaying much hostile feeling; but their power did not extend to destroy it completely, nor to banish to the domain of the past the fatal struggles to which angry passions give birth. Much more is needed to eradicate the evil, and to unite for ever the interests of two classes which have been so long divided.

Co-operative societies seem destined to take an important part in bringing about this salutary revolution. Many other institutions, by encouraging thrift, have greatly improved the working-man's condition; but co-operative societies,—that is, co-operative societies *for production*,—have the effect of transforming him directly into a capitalist, by securing to him a share in the profits of the undertaking in which he has invested the capital of his labour. The failure of some of these attempts has brought the whole system into, we think, undeserved discredit. It will be interesting, therefore, to make known the success which, owing to judicious management, they have obtained in quarters where the greatest obstacles might have been anticipated. We choose two examples, provided, one by the researches of the Royal Commission, the other by a report on the population in the agricultural districts, presented last year to Parliament. The first shows the co-operative system as applied to one of the trades requiring the largest amount of capital, viz., the working of a colliery; the other shows it as applied to agriculture.

THE COLLIERY OF BRIGGS AND COMPANY.

A floating capital, of about 100*l.* for every man employed, is necessary to make a colliery pay. No association, therefore, composed exclusively of working miners could command sufficient capital to carry on such an undertaking. How many years would it be before they could accumulate 100*l.* apiece? And even then, how could they give up their regular wage, which alone insures them their daily bread, in return for a dividend which, in so uncertain a trade, might one year be large, and the year following nothing at all? These difficulties, apparently insurmountable, have been overcome in the happiest manner by the system adopted in Mr. Briggs' collieries. Struck by its advantages, the Commission examined not only the founders of the business, but likewise several workmen, who, from being their bitterest enemies, have now become their associates and most active assistants.

The Whitwood and Methley Junction Collieries are situated in South Yorkshire, where, as we have shown, war, with strikes on one side and lock-out on the other, has been carried on incessantly of late years with intense animosity. These pits have probably suffered more from these causes than any others that could be named. Mr. Toft, one of the workman-shareholders in the present society, told the Commission that, in 1863, at one of the meetings, at which the Union orators did their best to inflame the passions of an audience already exasperated against the masters, he himself exclaimed, "If Mr. Briggs only had horns on, he would be the very devil." Mr. Briggs himself probably had not a much better opinion of these popular leaders, for he was chairman of an association of masters formed for the sole purpose of resisting the Unions.

It was in the midst of these struggles that he resolved to try a great experiment, and to see whether, giving up the plan of attacking them openly, he might not render the existence of these societies unnecessary, by offering the workmen advantages greater than any the Unions had ever been able to promise them. The property in the colliery, valued at about 90,000*l.*, was made over to a joint-stock company, and divided into 9,000 shares of 10*l.* each.* The original proprietors retained two-thirds of the capital, in order to secure to themselves the direction of the concern; the remaining 3,000 shares were offered to the miners, to their own customers, and to the public. The workmen thus had the chance offered them of becoming proprietors; but they would not have been able to take advantage of it unless they had also been furnished with the means of procuring this capital of 10*l.*, and unless a stronger attraction than the small dividend thence arising had been held out to them.

With this view, Mr. Briggs discarded the mystery which most manufacturers like to throw over the amount of their profits, and resolved to share them with his workmen, in order to interest them as much as possible

---

* A little later the number of shares was raised by a fresh issue to 10,000.—*Author's Note.*

in the success of the business. The funds of the company were regarded as divided into two parts, of which one was the imaginary capital represented by the labour of the miners, the other was the sum actually invested in shares. Under this arrangement, the wages, which were paid on the same scale as in the neighbouring collieries, represented the interest secured to the workmen on the first of these two capitals; and, as regards the second, it was settled that the shareholders should have ten per cent. interest on the receipts—a very fair profit when it is considered that it was to cover the deficit of bad years, in which the investor made nothing, whereas the payment of the wages is never suspended. It was provided that any excess, after making these two deductions from the profits, should be regarded as the common property of the whole society, and be divided equally between the workmen and shareholders. If, for instance, the net profits on the share capital amounted in any year to fourteen per cent., ten per cent. would be considered as interest on capital, together with two per cent. additional by way of bonus, and the remaining two per cent. would go to the workmen, among whom it would be divided in proportion to the amount of wages earned by each in the course of the year.*

* By taking the sum total of a workman's wages in the course of a year as the interest on the imaginary capital represented by his labour, we arrive at the amount of this capital. Supposing a workman to earn 50*l*. in a year, and calculating interest at the rate of 10 per cent. as on the share capital, his capital would be 500*l*.—*Author's Note.*

In order, however, to encourage them to become members of the society, an advantage has, up to this time, been allowed in the division of extra profits to the men holding shares. For instance, in 1866 these workmen received ten per cent., and the others only five per cent., on the annual amount of their wages. This difference was re-adjusted in 1867, and it was then settled that, in the division of the bonus, the part allotted to the shareholding workmen should represent twelve per cent., and that to the others eight per cent. on their wages.

The system was put in force in July, 1865. Most of the Union leaders had promised to support Mr. Briggs in his experiment, but they could not overcome the distrust of the workmen. The mere word Union exerted such a fascination over their minds, that they could not be persuaded to give it up, even for an institution in every way preferable. Mr. Briggs made a rule that every man who wished to participate in the bonus should buy a little book, costing only a penny, in which his wages should be entered every week; so great was their distrust, and so firmly were they convinced that the advantage offered them was only a snare, that only one-third of the workmen would go to this trifling expense. It is needless to say that when, on the 1st of January, 1867, all those who could produce a book received five per cent. more than those who could not, these prejudices vanished never to return. Nevertheless, from the incurable indifference which so many people show to their own interests, a tenth part of the workmen to this day neglect this simple formality.

Nothing can afford a better proof of the success achieved by Mr. Briggs and his brother,* than the figures submitted to the Commission. In the year 1867 they realized a net profit of 20,417*l.* after paying all outlays and allowing for wear and tear. A portion only of this sum was divided,—8,000*l.* was laid by in order to secure a bonus to the men in the bad years that might come. Though this happened to be a period of great prosperity in the coal trade, still the result is not the less remarkable; for, in Mr. Briggs' opinion, the old system would not have yielded equal profits under similar circumstances. And what is still more remarkable, the yield of the mine, owing to the new arrangements introduced by the society, was hardly at all affected by the subsequent period of depression. A different spirit moved all the workers in it; the interests of all were identified with the success of the undertaking, they laboured at the accomplishment of their task no longer with the indifference of the hireling, but with

---

* The late Mr. Henry Briggs, the former Chairman of the Coal Owners' Association, the father of the two gentlemen referred to in the text, was the head of the firm at the time of the conversion of the business into an industrial partnership. He died in the spring of this year, after witnessing the complete success of his great undertaking.— *Editor's Note.*

all the eagerness of the proprietor in pursuit of fortune. There have been no more strikes, and only six days, during which working has been stopped, in the course of three years; when a reduction of wages has been necessary, a few explanations have sufficed to make it accepted without a murmur. On one occasion the workmen in one of the pits having asked for an increase of pay, the Messrs. Briggs consulted the rest of the miners, who unanimously decided against it. Thenceforth the workmen were trusted to keep watch over all the petty details, which ensure economy and good management in all large establishments, but especially in a business in which wages come to seventy per cent. of the whole expenditure; and they performed their duty better than the most active inspectors. "When in the galleries," said one of them to us, "we see a nail on the ground we pick it up, repeating the words which have passed into a proverb, so much more towards the bonus at the end of the year." The men, who had been leaders of the Unions, are foremost in condemning and attacking the few who remain wedded to their old errors; and, being all shareholders, they are the most ardent defenders of the unequal division of the bonus. This question was argued between them and Mr. Briggs at one of the meetings of the Commission. Mr. Briggs was in favour of establishing an uniform division between all the workmen, whether shareholders or not; he maintained that, inasmuch as each man contributes a certain amount of labour to the common work, he has a right to a dividend exactly in proportion to the capital represented by his labour. His opponents, less influenced by any ideas of abstract right than by the good effects produced by unequal distribution, replied that it was above all things important at the present time to induce the workmen to become capitalists; and, therefore, that every encouragement ought to be held out to them to take shares in the society. The system of division of profits gave all of them the means of doing so; those who refused did not do so much to keep up the business as the others, and, consequently, had no right to the same advantages. The advantage in favour of the shareholder was all the more necessary, because the mere dividend on one share represents only the wages of a good workman for three or four days, and would never be sufficient inducement for him to save penny by penny the necessary 10l. He would never submit to this wholesome self-denial unless he could, at the same time, make sure of a larger share in the profits of his labour. "He has to learn," they say, "the advantages of becoming a capitalist; he does not know what they are. Well; here is a very good opportunity for giving him a little of that compulsory education, about which there is so much talk at the present day."

Experience will teach us which of the two systems is best. Without deciding between them, we have quoted this argument in order to show how completely, in their anxiety for the success of their common enterprise, both masters and men have shaken off all caste prejudices. Thanks to the spirit thus engendered, thrifty habits are increasing among the workmen. At the end of 1867 a thousand of them shared in the bonus, only three of whom spent it in drink, and these were dismissed with the unanimous approbation of their companions. For a society so recently established the number of working shareholders is considerable, being 144 out of 989 adult workmen; they hold 178 shares, equivalent to 1,780*l.*; an important capital, considering that it represents the three years' savings of men till then strangers to all ideas of economy.* They have every facility afforded them for acquiring the shares: all those upon which they have paid an instalment of 3*l.* are secured to them;† and, out of the last issue, 230 were reserved especially for the workpeople. The prosperity of the society is so great that the shares

* The shares are distributed as follows:—Out of 785 workmen, who labour underground, 83 are the holders of 94 shares, while among the top or surface workmen, only 204 in number, 84 shares are held among 61 men. One man is a holder of six shares among both the top and the underground workmen.—*Author's Note.*

† The shares thus bought by instalments have all been fully paid up: not a single instance has occurred of a workman failing in this respect.—*Author's Note.*

are already at 4*l*. 10*s*. premium : under these circumstances, the reservation of shares has proved an important advantage to the workmen, for they are allowed to purchase them at 12*l*. 5*s*., which is 2*l*. 5*s*. below the market price. In addition to the above named, nine managers, clerks, &c., hold 86 shares, 114 are held by non-resident agents of the Company, 1,878 by the public, and 1,068 by customers. These last, owing to their own interests being involved in the prosperity of the business, have done their very best, in times of slackness, to keep up the yield of the pits, and consequently of the profits also.

These results, remarkable as they are, give but a faint idea of the progress accomplished under the influence of this system. The material profits gained by the proprietors and the workmen are trifling in comparison with the other benefits which it has secured them; that is to say, the harmony, peace, and mutual sympathy which now reign where so lately hatred and distrust embittered every heart. The Messrs. Briggs have, as they expected, seen the Union virtually broken up, without any overt act of hostility on their part. Never have they refused to engage a man because he belonged to it; but its members, seeing clearly that it was no longer wanted, have of their own accord abandoned it, so that in Mr. Briggs' colliery, in which in 1865 almost all the workmen were members of the

Union, about forty only remain faithful to it, and these with no other motive than the wish to live in peace with their neighbours.

Nevertheless the work, so happily begun, is not yet finished : it is to be hoped that gradually all the workmen will become shareholders, and even take an important part in the management of the business. The founders are anxious that they should; the hesitation is rather on the part of the working shareholders, who think they have not yet acquired sufficient experience to justify them in undertaking so important a trust.*

THE ASSINGTON AGRICULTURAL SOCIETY.

The second example which we propose to quote is that of a *bonâ fide* co-operative society applied to agriculture. It has not attracted much attention, though it deserves to be well known; for it possesses the authority of thirty-eight years' experience attended with constant success, in spite of the difficulties and uncertainties which always accompany farming operations.

Mr. Gurdon, a landed proprietor in the neighbourhood of the village of Assington in Norfolk, started this

---

* Others, besides Messrs. Briggs, have adopted this system. The same principle has been carried out in Greening's manufacture of articles in iron at Middlesborough, and at the iron-works of Fox and Head, at Salford. But, by a succession of adverse circumstances, these two establishments have not yet been able to declare a dividend.—*Author's Note.*

society. In 1830 he let sixty acres of middling land to an association of fifteen labourers, who assumed the name of the Assington Co-operative Agricultural Society. Each one contributed the small sum of 3*l*., which, with an advance of 400*l*. from Mr. Gurdon, made up the society's capital. Only the inhabitants of the parish can hold shares, and if they leave it, they must dispose of their interest. There is not regular work on the farm for more than five men and two or three boys; nevertheless, one of the rules is, that only shareholders shall be employed, and that no outsiders shall be called in, unless more hands are wanted than they can supply. One of the labourers is entrusted with the general management of the farm, and receives an allowance of a shilling a week, as agent, in addition to his regular wages. The financial business is conducted by a committee of four members, two of whom are re-elected every year. Although the capital of the society did not reach the figure which English farmers consider necessary in order to do justice to the land, yet it prospered; it added 130 acres to the farm, and, in order to meet its expenses, of which rent came in for 200*l*., it took in six more shareholders. The loan from Mr. Gurdon was repaid; the society became the owner of all the farm stock, comprising six horses, four cows, a hundred and ten sheep, and thirty pigs; it insured its buildings for 500*l*., and at last the three pounds shares rose in the market to the extraordinary price of 50*l.*, more than sixteen times their original value.

So good an example was sure to be followed, and in 1854 a similar society was established in the neighbourhood on rather a larger scale, and seems likely to do as well.* This application by labourers of the co-operative system to agriculture seems to be worthy of notice. Its success, when conducted with judgment, proves how effectual it is, and how fertile in results; and its example may tend to weaken the artificial distinction which often in our country separates the country from the town workman. Although the situation of the agricultural labourer is very precarious, often very trying in England, it is evident that he has succeeded in establishing an institution, which many people treated as a visionary scheme. Agriculture is with us, far more than on the other side of the Channel, the most important national industry. The diversities between the artizan and the labourer, arising from the different conditions of their lives, do not prevent their interests from being identical. The artizan has better opportunities of instruction, greater facilities for united action, both the generous emotions and the hasty impulses of

---

* Many co-operative societies exist in America, in trades requiring considerable capital. Several were mentioned to the Commission; among them, one for working a colliery in Illinois, and a co-operative foundry at Troy, in the State of New York, which yields a very fair profit.—*Author's Note.*

his mind are quickened by a life spent in great cities : he is capable therefore of furnishing to the labourer both an example of noble deeds to be imitated, and a warning against dangers to be avoided; on the other hand, he may learn many a useful lesson in return from the race of men whose daily labour through so many generations has fertilized our soil.

Each wants the qualities, that can be imparted by the other, to complete them both. The national character of the French people is in a great measure composed of the combination of these two elements; they are at the same time laborious and ingenious, equally suited to hard labour in the field, and to the refined inventions of modern science. Our nation is eager to take up every noble cause, yet proud, sometimes even exclusive in its patriotism ; in defence of its honour it quickly recovers all its energies, even after the most cruel deceptions and the greatest discouragement, and it is ready to submit to any sacrifice, if, instead of being blindly led and treated with suspicion, it is allowed to feel itself the free champion of liberal ideas; the versatility of its genius affords it peculiar fitness for confidently taking up and striving to fathom the grave questions to which we have drawn attention, and for seeking the practical solution of some of the most important problems which the future has in store for us.

CHAPTER X.

POLITICAL LIBERTY AND THE FUTURE PROSPECTS OF UNIONS.

WE have left far behind us the sad scenes at Sheffield. The reader will ere this have perceived why we did not shrink from exposing them in all their horror: it was the best means of proving that the most important Unions were in no way connected with, or answerable for these crimes. It has been seen that after the great industrial conflicts which these societies have maintained against the masters, they have more than once assisted in restoring a good understanding between employers and workmen, either by becoming sureties for a real treaty of peace concluded between them, or by yielding their place to new associations of improved form. But their task should not stop there; and their leaders, pleading for them before the Royal Commission, have shown to it the new part, which they discern, reserved for the societies which they represent.

On the day when the law shall permit them to hold property by corporate title, when boards of arbitration, rendering nearly all strikes useless, shall leave unemployed the funds which their barren cost has till now absorbed, they will have something better to do than to dissolve themselves: they will be able themselves to become the nucleus of the co-operative societies, whose pacific action is destined to replace their agitated reign. For indeed these great Unions, which extend all over England, whose budgets every year amount to thousands upon thousands of pounds, will then have at their disposal the two elements which are indispensable to the success of such undertakings: a strong organization, and a capital capable of insuring credit. To the absence of these two elements is to be attributed the downfall of most co-operative societies; and it is to be hoped that the Unions will know some day how to employ their vast resources in resuming the task under far more favourable circumstances than their predecessors.

But we are willing to dispense with this hypothesis: we do not need it. For a fair trial has already proved the value of the remedies, which we have seen so successfully applied towards mitigating the feeling of antagonism between masters and men, the cause of so much suffering.

Among all these remedies there is one which we hold to be most powerful and most indispensable, one to which we would especially call attention. It is not once mentioned in any of the ten volumes of reports published by the Commission, though it is familiar to all the persons who figure in them, and it is impossible to read two lines of that vast collection of evidence without detecting its influence. We have not quoted a single fact in the course of this investigation which does not bear witness to the power and the necessity of that influence. We need hardly say that the specific to which we are alluding, and at which the reader must have already guessed, is political liberty, and the various rights secured by it; and, first, the right of writing and publishing, which England enjoys, and the wide notoriety which sheds upon all questions the most searching light. The Commission had only to throw open its doors to call forth a discussion so free and so beneficial, that more than once those who entered as opponents departed reconciled. The heavy stamp-duties which in France confine the use of political papers to a comparatively small number, and thus render them a luxury attainable only by a few, can only tend to lower the intellects; the press in England is entirely free, and is, therefore, able to distribute at a low price numerous publications, in which nothing is omitted that can interest the country, and the mass of the people are enlightened by the constant and serious discussion of public affairs.

On the other hand, the right of meeting, which is

exercised as naturally and as completely as the right of way on the high road, allows all ideas, all aspirations, to appear in broad daylight, and to be expressed without disguise, while, at the same time, it submits them to the critical test of public opinion. Accordingly, the Unions are in the habit of meeting on all occasions; but, taught by experience, they seldom discuss abstract questions; they assemble only for the purpose of transacting their own affairs. These practical discussions create opportunities by which the men most fitted to take the lead are brought into notice. The public is invited to their deliberations with the view of exciting its interest, and dispelling its mistrust. No one disputes this right, not even when they use it in the most threatening manner; as on the day when more than 20,000 men, all members of Unions, were seen marching in close ranks with flying colours to take part in a great political demonstration. The police interfered only for the purpose of preventing the carriage traffic from disturbing the long procession.*

Such liberty has doubtless favoured both the formation and the increase of Unions; but the most timid minds can hardly regret this, as the result has been the disappearance from the soil of England of the secret societies, which used to flourish there as well as on the

---

* The destruction of the Hyde Park railings, which happened a short time afterwards, was the work of the London roughs; the Unionists were in no way concerned in it.—*Author's Note.*

Continent. They have become useless, through the fact of everybody being allowed to claim openly all the advantages which their members could hope to gain by secret plotting. Theories most contrary to social order, as it is now understood, might be put forward any day with impunity, if an audience willing to listen to them could be assembled; but, on the other hand, the most ardent reformers reckon on legal means alone to achieve the triumph of their cause. The free institutions, by which the English are governed, enable them to trust to their own perseverance and to the national sense of equity for the redress of all grievances, which they believe to be well founded, and they know that conquests, which are the work of time, are much more durable than any that might be effected by violence. At the Congress of Lausanne a remarkable instance of this respect for the law occurred, and one akin to the present subject. The English delegates complained bitterly of the state of the law, which a few months previously had refused to grant protection to the funds of Unions, upon which the Congress proposed to pass a vote of censure upon the judges who gave the decision; but the Englishmen opposed this, saying that the law was unjust, and that they would do their best to get it changed, but that as long as it remained law, they must respect the judges who applied it.

From what was elicited as to the state of things in

England by the inquiries of the Royal Commission, we derive additional proof of the fact that the social progress of the working-classes, and the pacific solution of the great questions connected with that progress, are in all countries inseparably linked with political freedom. In all times the powers adverse to liberty have indulged in the belief that they could either smother these questions, or turn to their own profit the passions which they arouse. They have claimed the credit of protecting the rich classes against popular excesses by silence; and of furthering the interests of the working-classes, by the interposition of their authority, better than they could have done so themselves : a double and fatal mistake, pregnant with cruel disappointment for the people which allows itself to cherish such a delusion. The absence of publicity and of free discussion envenoms, does not solve, the questions which it may for a time succeed in keeping in the background, and in the end is sure to create a gulf between the various classes comprising the same nation. Such questions ought to be treated like the coal-mines we have already mentioned, in which the subtlest poison mingles with inexhaustible treasures : if the air is excluded, the deadly gas accumulates ; but if the mines are well ventilated, the greatest motive-power of modern industry may be extracted from them without danger.

Those who have most cause to fear the explosion of

popular passions are the parties most interested in not allowing them to ferment under cover of darkness. That kind of half liberty is equally mischievous which permits theories to be answered only by counter assertions; chimerical dreams only by irrelevant dissertations on the subject of abstract rights; which gives people the useless right of speaking, but refuses to allow them any practical influence in the conduct of their affairs; and which is an obstacle to the constant intercourse whereby asperities are softened and juster ideas of truth acquired. This kind of liberty is favourable only to the development of extreme opinions. Debilitated eyes, accustomed to this dangerous twilight, are easily deceived; a sort of deception that may be compared to the effect produced by those coloured glasses through which we sometimes look at a landscape. A light brilliant as that of the sun, and, like it, composed of innumerable different hues, is needed to arrive at a right understanding of political and social questions; such a light can proceed only from the full and free expression of public opinion in all its shapes.

Political liberty is not less necessary to the working classes. Without its aid how are they to appreciate their true interests? How are they to separate truth from falsehood, the practical from the unpractical in the language of those who court their favour? How are they to exercise the just influence to which they are entitled on public opinion? Lastly, what security have they for the enjoyment of the legitimate improvements which they have obtained, and for those which they still demand? Political freedom is the parent of all other liberty, and alone can give strength and life to the principle of association,—a hardy plant, which loves the open air, and cannot live or bear fruit under glass. But for the various rights, which they have used so largely, Trade Unions would have continued for ever to be mere engines of war, capable of prolonging contests fatal to the workmen themselves, but ill fitted for securing them any permanent benefits. Though the workmen are now in the peaceful enjoyment of these rights, which are common to all Englishmen, yet they take just as great an interest, as the other classes of society in political questions. Their present and special object is to get rid of the legal obstacles, which are still suffered in some degree to interfere with their right of association. Yet quite recently, when the extension of the franchise became the question of the day, they clearly showed how deeply they valued that important reform. They know besides that, though the Liberal party may in most cases enter best into their feelings and understand their wants, yet in all parties they are sure to find statesmen, worthy of the name, always ready to listen to them, and to devote themselves to the defence of their interests.

In France, unfortunately, these social questions have always been stirred up at times of great political crises, the most unfavourable moment for their solution, when minds are disturbed, passions inflamed, and material prosperity rudely shaken. But such questions are too nearly connected with the sources of national grandeur to be long deprived of the light thrown upon them by political liberty, especially in a country, all whose institutions are founded on universal suffrage, the sovereign judge who can always reverse his own decrees. In France where that judge is the recognised organ of popular will, where none can dispute his authority, and where all causes worthy of prevailing in the national councils, and all legitimate grievances, reckon on invoking his past decisions as warnings for the future, these questions cannot fail to touch him most deeply, and the day will come when he will make use of the power conferred on him in seeking their solution. Liberty and publicity, the only safe guarantees for justice, are as necessary to the tribunal of Universal Suffrage as to any other court; these two only can blot out the traces of those terrible misunderstandings which have raised such alarm in some, so many vain illusions in others, which have caused so much blood to flow, and have left in the hearts of men those two fatal consequences of civil war, cowardly weakness and intense hatred. Liberty and publicity can alone prevent, if there were any reason to fear it, the recurrence of similar disasters.

Therefore, in showing the influence of political liberty on social questions in England, we believe that we have brought forward an encouraging example for those who are interested in the future of the same questions in France. Would it be wise to neglect this lesson, under the idea that, owing to the peculiarities of the British Constitution, experiments conducted under its protection would be unsafe in France? We think not, and that this would be exaggerating the importance of the ancient and complicated machinery of which it is composed. Constitutions, however artfully framed, are invariably governed by one ruling power; one, in which really independent and opposite influences stood exactly balanced against one another, would be shattered by their shock, like a machine subjected to contrary forces. It is not any particular clause, unknown elsewhere, which has sustained the English Constitution in the midst of all the political and social revolutions of our age; it is the power which is destined to wield sovereign authority in all free countries, and that power is public opinion. However much the institutions, by means of which the power of opinion makes itself felt, may vary in all these countries, they may always be compared to translations of one and the same thought in different languages.

Why should we French, and we alone, be condemned to have no terms in our language by which to express it? We are not more excluded than others from the political liberty, to which every race and every country have a right. The remedy afforded by political liberty against the dangers arising out of social questions is equally effectual among all nations, who are competent to apply it; and no people, jealous of maintaining its rank in the world, can now with impunity treat this liberty, the highest attribute of civilized man, as a mere ornament, to be worn to-day, and on the morrow cast aside with disdain.

APPENDIX.*

The following are the calculations of Mr. Finlaison as to the solvency of the two societies whose balance-sheets were submitted to his examination :—

In ordinary Friendly Societies, 100,000 men, admitted at the age of eighteen, would, by the time the survivors had attained sixty years of age, be reduced to 52,489 by mortality only. But secession from the society, combined with mortality, will have reduced them to 29,297. The importance, therefore, of this element in the calculations is clear.

It is estimated that the average age of members of the Amalgamated Society of Engineers at this moment is thirty-five. On reaching sixty the members acquire a right to the superannuation allowance; at the same time they naturally cease to have any claim to sick allowance; and, on the other hand, also cease to pay subscriptions. The subscriptions, therefore, are in the nature of a life annuity, terminating at the age of sixty. The society consists of 32,720 subscribing members.

The society guarantees each member ten shillings a week during sickness, and the reduction in this sum at the end of twenty-six weeks, being balanced by that granted as compensation in case of accident, the sick allowance is at the rate of 16,360*l.* per week assured to all members. The average

* See page 50.

pension in old age being taken at 20*l.* 16*s.* per annum, it follows that under this head the sum of 680,576*l.* is assured to the whole body: and 12*l.* assured on the death of each member will give 392,640*l.* to be paid sooner or later. Lastly, the funds are already charged with pensions in course of payment to the amount of 5,232*l.*

Valued according to the tables of mortality and sickness used by Friendly Societies, these charges may be represented by the following statement :—

LIABILITIES.

	£
16,360*l.*, weekly allowance in sickness until 60	355,339
680,576*l.*, per annum, pensions for life after 60	1,985,512
392,640*l.*, sums payable on death	168,167
5,232*l.*, pensions in course of payment	44,697
Total liabilities	2,553,715

ASSETS.

	£
85,072*l.* yearly contribution, payable until 60	1,254,395
1,636*l.* weekly contribution, suspended during sickness, reducing the first by	35,534
Remainder	1,218,861
Tangible assets in hand	138,113
Arrears	10,068
Total assets	1,367,042

	£
Total liabilities capitalized	2,553,715
Total assets capitalized	1,367,042
Deficit	1,186,673

But by degrees Mr. Finlaison reduces this deficit to its true value; he begins by taking into consideration the effect of secessions.

Assuming, in order to make up the annual contribution of 2*l.* 12*s.*, that these secessions are in the same proportion as in Friendly Societies, and making deductions for the ordinary chances of sickness, during which payment of subscription ceases, it will be found that the annual subscription is represented by a capital of 33*l*. 18*s*. 9*d*., which, multiplied by 32,720, the number of subscribing members, gives the sum of 1,110,468*l*. as the capital of the society. By applying a similar calculation to the reduction in expenditure consequent on secessions, we arrive at a different statement of liabilities and assets, viz.,

LIABILITIES.

		£
Capital representing sick allowance		322,612
,, ,, superannuation allowance		1,633,586
,, ,, funeral expenses		151,330
,, ,, pensions in course of payment		44,688*
Total liabilities		2,152,216

ASSETS.

	£
By present value of contributions payable, or actual capital of society	1,110,468
Tangible assets and arrears	148,181
Total assets	1,258,649

	£
Total liabilities capitalized	2,152,216
Total assets capitalized	1,258,649
Deficit	893,567

The three first items of liability in the first statement amount to 2,509,018*l*. The same three first items of liability in the second statement amount to 2,107,528*l*. A difference, therefore, of 401,490*l*. is obtained by taking the secessions into consideration.

But Mr. Finlaison shows that the average number of secessions in ordinary Friendly Societies, on which this calculation is founded, represents only two-fifths of the average of secessions as shown by the statistical tables of the society. In

* It is not clear why Mr. Finlaison puts pensions here at 44,688*l*., and at 44,697*l*. in the previous statement.—*Author's Note.*

order, therefore, to arrive at the real reduction in liability produced by secessions, the amount 401,490*l.* must be augmented in the same proportion, that is, to 1,003,725*l.*; or put algebraically, $401{,}490 : x :: 2 : 5, \frac{401{,}490 \times 5}{2} = 1{,}003{,}725$, and this is the object of the last rectification. In fact the sum of 1,003,725*l.*, as caused by secession, ought to be taken off the first valuation of liabilities put at 2,553,715*l.*, thus reducing liabilities to 1,549,990*l.* This increase in the secession valuation reduces the capital of the society to the sum of 947,879*l.*, without affecting the tangible assets and arrears, amounting to 148,181*l.*; the assets, therefore, are brought up to the sum of 1,096,060*l.* We then arrive at the following result:—

	£
Reduced liabilities	1,549,990
Assets	1,096,060
Deficit reduced to	453,930

This is the deficit which an addition of sixpence to the weekly subscription would be sufficient to cover; for the capital of the society would by this means be increased to half as much again as what it now is, and the assets would show the following figures:—

	£
Present capital, represented by 1*s.* a week subscriptions	947,879
Sixpence a week additional	473,940
Tangible assets and arrears	148,181
Total assets	1,570,000
Liabilities	1,549,990
Surplus of assets over liabilities	20,010

In this calculation Mr. Finlaison supposes all the resources of the society to have been spent in benefits. The outgoing for donations to members out of employment will, however, make a difference in the result arrived at in the last statement. But even taking this expense at his valuation, we cannot be contented with expressing the hope, never to be realised, that Unions will renounce strikes, which are the special objects of their existence; on the contrary, we will endeavour to calculate, by means of his own figures, in what manner they may in future meet this important expense without danger.

Judging from their own statistics, Mr. Finlaison says that these donations may be reckoned as double the amount spent in sick allowance. This allowance, represented in the second of the foregoing statements by a capital of 322,612*l.*, was found, on increasing by two-fifths the secession valuation, to be reduced to a capital of 273,521*l.*, so that double this last sum, 547,042*l.*, will express in round numbers the capital representing the average of strike expenses for sixteen years, during which numerous and protracted contests have occurred. This figure, less the surplus of 20,010*l.* given above, denotes the deficit which the Union will have to provide for, even after having raised the subscription to eighteen-pence a week, if, as there is no reason to doubt it will, it persists in allowing strike expenses to figure as the most considerable of its outgoings: they would amount to 527,032*l.*

There are various ways in which these expenses might be met:—

I. By a superadded increase of sixpence three farthings to the weekly subscription, which would raise it to two shillings and three farthings. The deficit amounts to 527,032*l.*, and this fresh addition to the subscriptions would represent a capital of 524,181*l.*, thereby reducing the deficit to 2,851*l.*

II. If, as is probable, this contribution, which would amount to 5*l.* 7*s.* 3*d.* a year, were too large for the small means of a workman, a more simple, more practical, and more logical method would be to leave the subscription at eighteen-pence a week, and to diminish the rate of the different benefits granted by the society.

The amount spent in benefits by the society was, in the last statement, represented by a capital of 1,549,990*l*., that spent in strikes by 547,042*l*., total 2,097,032*l*. By diminishing one quarter the charges for relief and allowances, a saving will be obtained which will go nearly as far to establish the equilibrium as the proposed superaddition to the subscription. Thus:—

	£
Deficit	527,032
Expenses reduced one quarter	524,258
Deficit reduced to	2,774

III. It would, perhaps, be still better to combine both systems, so as in some measure to obtain compensation for the effects produced by each. Thus:—

	£
By adding 3¼*d*. to the subscription, making it 1*s*. 9¼*d*. a week, the receipts would be increased by a sum represented by a capital of	256,717
By reducing the benefit expenses one-eighth, a saving would be effected represented by	262,129
Total	518,846

The result of this would be,—

	£
Deficit	527,032
Gain by increase and saving	518,846
Reducing the deficit to	8,186

And if the funeral expenses alone were reduced another eighth, that is to say, brought down from 12*l*. to 9*l*., a fresh saving of 12,794*l*. would be effected, and this would assure a surplus of 4,608*l*.

POSTSCRIPT.

At a time like the present, when disputes between the pitmen and colliery proprietors have been causing bloodshed almost simultaneously in Wales, in the Charleroi district of Belgium, and in the valley of the Loire in France, the success of the experiment tried by the Messrs. Briggs is particularly interesting. We have much satisfaction, therefore, in announcing that, during the past year, their success, instead of growing less, has surpassed their expectations. A profit larger than that of any of the preceding years was divided on the 1st of January, 1869. But, in these times of distrust and agitation, it is the moral results of the experiment that it is most important to notice. Accordingly, the annexed document, of which we have just received a copy, is of a nature especially to interest our readers. It shows with what perfect good faith the workmen have met the equally well-meant advances of the Messrs. Briggs, and that, casting aside the long-cherished feelings of animosity as completely as their employers have discarded traditional prejudices, they now afford them powerful and hearty support. The openly-declared hostility of several colliery proprietors to the principle of industrial partnership occasioned the meeting to be held. Indeed, although the effects of the system have been considerably to increase the actual profits of the capitalists who have adopted it, nevertheless, it must naturally appear a dangerous innovation to all those who look upon any attempt at identifying the interests of masters and workmen as a visionary scheme. Accordingly, the experiment has been viewed with extreme suspicion by most of the establishments in the neighbourhood of the Messrs. Briggs, and it appears that the directors of one of these collieries have recently announced their intention of entering into a competitive contest with Messrs. Briggs, in the course of which they expect to see the Whitwood Company fall to pieces, and with its fall to put an end to the whole system which gives them offence. It was to meet these threats that the principal workmen of the Messrs. Briggs held a meeting on the 17th of June, at which, on the suggestion of two of their number, Mr. Black and Mr. Toft, the following resolution was carried unanimously :—" That the workmen assembled at this meeting, in view of the opposition to the industrial partnership principle openly avowed by the proprietors of a neighbouring colliery, desire to express their confidence in the directors and managers of Henry Briggs, Son, & Co., Limited ; and resolve to use their utmost endeavours to strengthen their hands by thorough co-operation, in entire confidence that no sacrifice will be required from the workmen unless absolutely necessary to defeat that opposition."

The above was proposed by D. Black, seconded by J. Toft, and carried unanimously.

Mr. Briggs draws attention to the fact that Mr. Toft, the seconder of this resolution, is the same man who a few years ago described his father as " the very devil."

Twickenham, 21*st June.*

THE END.

London : Printed by SMITH, ELDER & Co., Old Bailey, E.C.

www.ingramcontent.com/pod-product-compliance
Lightning Source LLC
Chambersburg PA
CBHW032205230426
43672CB00011B/2519